*THE LIGHT
FROM BEHIND
THE SUN*

THE LIGHT FROM BEHIND THE SUN

—

A REFORMED & EVANGELICAL APPRECIATION OF C.S. LEWIS

—

DOUGLAS WILSON

The Light from Behind the Sun: A Reformed and Evangelical Appreciation of C.S. Lewis
Copyright © 2021 by Douglas Wilson
Published by Canon Press
P. O. Box 8729, Moscow, Idaho 83843
800-488-2034 | www.canonpress.com

Cover design by James Engerbretson.
Interior design by Valerie Anne Bost.

All rights reserved. No part of this publication may be reproduced, stored in a retrieval system, or transmitted in any form by any means, electronic, mechanical, photocopy, recording, or otherwise, without prior permission of the author, except as provided by USA copyright law.

Unless otherwise indicated, all Scripture quotations are from the King James (Authorized) Version. Bible quotations marked ESV are from the English Standard Version English Standard Version, copyright ©2001 by Crossway Bibles, a division of Good News Publishers. Used by permission..

Library of Congress Cataloging-in-Publication Data:
Wilson, Douglas, 1953- author.
The light from behind the sun : a reformed and evangelical appreciation of C.S. Lewis / Douglas Wilson.
Moscow, Idaho : Canon Press, [2021]
LCCN 2021022597 | ISBN 9781954887152 (paperback)
Subjects: LCSH: Lewis, C. S. (Clive Staples), 1898-1963.
Classification: LCC BX4827.L44 W55 2021 | DDC 230.092—dc23
LC record available at https://lccn.loc.gov/2021022597

22 23 24 25 26 27 28 29   10 9 8 7 6 5 4 3 2 1

CONTENTS

	Introduction	1
1	Lewis Gets It Wrong	3
2	The Absence of Susan	9
3	The Curious Presence of Emeth	33
4	The Light From Behind the Sun.	51
5	The Tao of Lewis	77
6	Undragoned—C.S. Lewis on the Gift of Salvation.	95
7	Was C.S. Lewis Reformed?	119
8	The Ransom Trilogy	135
9	The Shadow of that Hyddeous Strength. .	143
10	Hell and Damnation	163

11 Tongues of Angels 177

12 Children without Chests 185

13 Lewis and the Eccentric Creationist 195

INTRODUCTION

I don't often use *the kingdom, the power, and the glory*. When I do, I have an idea of the *kingdom* as sovereignty *de jure*; God, as good, would have a claim on my obedience even if He had no power. The *power* is the sovereignty *de facto*—He is omnipotent. And the *glory* is—well, the glory; the "beauty so old and new," the "light from behind the sun." (*Letters to Malcolm*)[1]

This is a true miscellany. I have been reading Lewis for a number of decades, and once I became a writer, it should not be surprising I have been writing about him, also for decades. A few years ago, the thought occurred to me that I should put everything I had written on Lewis between two covers, and so

---

1. *Letters to Malcolm, Chiefly on Prayer* (1964; New York: Houghton Mifflin Harcourt, 2012), 28. All citations of C.S. Lewis works in this book are from the first referenced edition unless otherwise noted.

here we are. I wanted to do this as a way of honoring the intellectual debt I owe to Lewis. Although there are criticisms of him here, it would be fair to say that I owe more to Lewis in this regard than all other authors I have read put together—and this is saying something, because I owe *them* a lot.

The reader will be gracious to remember the disparate origins of these essays, and forgive a little repetition here and there. Where we noticed it, we gave it an editorial whack on the head, but I am sure some repetition got through anyhow. Some of it was addressed by combining or rearranging material, resulting in some significant differences from what was originally published. With all that said, please try to treat any repetition that you notice as something you needed to be reminded of (Phil. 3:1), and not an instance of us being tedious.

A portion of one of the articles was written for the magazine *Antithesis*. Another was a talk given at a Desiring God conference. One was a foreword to a book. Another was an article for the magazine *Credo*. Most of them were written for the blog *Blog and Mablog*. Special thanks should go to the owner of that blog, a fellow who has always treated me like a true gentleman.

DOUGLAS WILSON
Not anywhere near Oxford
Good Friday, 2021

CHAPTER 1
LEWIS GETS IT WRONG

Those who have read me for a long time know that I am a C.S. Lewis junkie. I have read and reread him, and have been edified by him in ways beyond reckoning. If I were to calculate the impact that various writers have had on me—and there have been many who have—he would always come in first, and by a large margin.

Even where you find my caveats—as in his early accommodations with evolution, or in the atrocious things he says about some of the psalms—I find myself simultaneously appalled and edified. For example, in *Reflections on the Psalms*, he says this:

> Still more in the Psalmists' tendency to chew over and over the cud of some injury, to dwell in a kind of self-torture on every circumstance that aggravates it, most of us can recognise something we have met

in ourselves. We are, after all, blood brothers to these ferocious, self-pitying, barbaric men.[1]

But still, reading through that book, which I think his worst, I find myself instructed and blessed at every turn. So go figure.

The problem lies with those Christians, like myself, who do not recoil from the imprecatory psalms in the same way that Lewis does. Lewis thinks that these psalms are included in God's Word as a sort of object lesson, a "don't try this at home, kids" kind of thing. "The ferocious parts of the Psalms serve as a reminder that there is in the world such a thing as wickedness and that it (if not its perpetrators) is hateful to God." (*Reflections on the Psalms*, 33).

As one of those who believe that we are to harmonize the imprecatory psalms with the rest of Scripture, and that we are to utilize them in our corporate worship and private devotions, I am afraid that Lewis would most likely regard me as a dangerous radical, as one who *likes* the permission to hate that such psalms seem to provide. I think he would find me on the wrong side of a caution he issued in another related respect.

> The hard sayings of our Lord are wholesome to those only who find them hard . . . . For there

---

1. *Reflections on the Psalms* (New York: Harcourt Brace, 1958), 26.

are two states of mind which face the Dominical paradoxes without flinching. God guard us from one of them.[2]

There are three quick reasons I would like to offer for suggesting that Lewis is wrong about this. I would like to persuade him that he should, after all, accept my Facebook friend request.

The first is that Lewis knows how to cut slack on this very same kind of issue, but the persons involved have to be in the New Testament. He alluded to the Lord's hard sayings in the quotation above. He recognizes the ferocity of the ancient psalmists in the Magnificat. But there he does what he ought to do with the psalms—say that there is a good way to emulate this, and a bad way to do so. I would argue that Lewis should follow his own example here.

Second, the apostles do not have the same attitude toward the imprecatory psalms that Lewis did. One of the fiercer ones is quoted by Peter when they are considering a replacement for Judas.

> For it is written in the book of Psalms, Let his habitation be desolate, and let no man dwell therein: and his bishoprick let another take. (Acts 1:20, see Psalm 69:25, and then Psalm 109:8)

---

2. C.S. Lewis, "The Dangers of National Repentance," *C.S. Lewis Essay Collection and Other Short Pieces*, ed. Lesley Walmsley (New York: HarperCollins, 2000), 296.

> Let his days be few; and let another take his office.
> Let his children be fatherless, and his wife a widow.
> Let his children be continually vagabonds, and beg:
> Let them seek their bread also out of their desolate places. (Psalm 109:8–10)

Psalm 109 is cited by Lewis as being one that was particularly bad. But if it were *that* bad, then why didn't Peter seem to recognize it? I believe that Lewis fell prey here to a common mistake, that of assuming the New Testament writers more or less "share" our world, as distinct from the ancients, when actually they were much closer to the ancients than they are to us.

And third, the New Testament does not invite us to divide the psalms into two categories, the kind that bless us and the kind that repulse us. We are simply sent to the undifferentiated psalms. "Is any among you afflicted? let him pray. Is any merry? let him sing psalms" (James 5:13). And the hymnbook of the Christian church is to be the entire psalter. "Speaking to yourselves in psalms and hymns and spiritual songs, singing and making melody in your heart to the Lord" (Eph. 5:19, cf. Col. 3:16).

So then, what? I would return to the caution Lewis gave in his essay on National Repentance. It is possible, in other words, to be scoring off some of your political enemies and at the same time feel like you are doing something that is personally humble and virtuous. Some people want to use the imprecatory psalms as a way of providing cover for their own personal anger issues. They want to break the teeth in *somebody's* jaw, and Psalm 3 provides them with a ready answer if rebuked for it. But there are others who understand that a hard world sometimes requires hard words. Lewis gets this when the Lord Himself delivers the hard words. But I think we can and should extend the principle.

CHAPTER 2
THE ABSENCE OF SUSAN

There are two things that really bother evangelical friends of Narnia, and they both show up in *The Last Battle*. One of them is the presence of Emeth in Aslan's country, and the other is the absence of Susan in that same country. The character of Emeth is a striking one, and the problem presented by him a significant one, worthy of a full treatment, so we will deal with it in the next essay.

What I would like to do here is address the troublesome absence of Susan from Aslan's country. What does it mean? Where does it fit in this story? Why does the apparent apostasy of Susan seem like a gaping narratival hole that doesn't fit with any part of the larger story? I want to argue that it does not seem to fit because it really doesn't fit. My intention is to show that a final apostasy on the part of Susan is really a literary impossibility.

I want to begin by sketching the character of Susan, as she is represented in the Narnia stories, beginning with what I take as clear indications of her faithfulness and loyalty. She is a true daughter. I then want to move on to discuss her characteristic failings and temptations. One of the things Lewis does throughout the Narnia stories is show how his child protagonists are fully capable of sins and failures, and Susan is no exception. So when she stumbles, how does she stumble?

From that point I want to move on to discuss the prophetic importance of Cair Paravel, and the nature of Cair Paravel (and all of Narnia), and how it all relates to Plato. Bless me, what do they teach them in these schools? And then, I want to sum up what I think happened to Susan.

So we begin with these four children. "Once there were four children whose names were Peter, Susan, Edmund and Lucy."[1] We will end with the same four.

TRUE DAUGHTER

There are many indications throughout the stories that Susan is an honest and sincere follower of Aslan. She can stumble, but when she does, Aslan

---

1. *The Lion, the Witch, and the Wardrobe* (1950; New York: Macmillan, 1970), 1.

puts things right again. "'Welcome, Peter, Son of Adam,' said Aslan. 'Welcome, Susan and Lucy'" (*The Lion*, 124). She is welcomed by the lion, and all is right.

She and Lucy are the two witnesses of the death of Aslan on the Stone Table. "'Please, may we come with you—wherever you're going?' asked Susan" (*The Lion*, 147). They accompany him there because he was hungry for the companionship. She clearly loves him: "'The cowards! The cowards!' sobbed Susan. 'Are they still afraid of him, even now?'" (*The Lion*, 151).

And together the two girls are the first witnesses of the resurrection. They held vigil all night after his death, and in the morning at sunrise, the table cracked in two, and Aslan was alive again. The Deeper Magic had undone all the witch's plans. "And he crouched down and the children climbed onto his warm, golden back, and Susan sat first, holding on tightly to his mane and Lucy sat behind holding on tightly to Susan" (*The Lion*, 161).

She was also the recipient of great gifts.

> "Susan, Eve's Daughter," said Father Christmas. "These are for you," and he handed her a bow and a quiver full of arrows and a little ivory horn. "You must use the bow only in great need," he said, "for I do not mean you to fight in the battle. It does not easily miss. And when you put this horn to your

lips and blow it, then, wherever you are, I think help of some kind will come to you." (*The Lion*, 104)

She grew into a great and beautiful queen, which will be discussed in a moment, but her carriage was not like that of a Jadis at all.

And Susan grew into a tall and gracious woman with black hair that fell almost to her feet and the kings of the countries beyond the sea began to send ambassadors asking for her hand in marriage. And she was called Susan the Gentle. (*The Lion*, 181)

When she was courted by Rabadash, more than a few have been struck by the fact that she gave that kind of character the time of day. But there was an explanation. Will she have him? "The lady shook her head. 'No, brother,' she said, 'not for all the jewels in Tashbaan.'"[2]

But why had she even thought about it?

"That was my folly, Edmund," said Queen Susan, "of which I cry you mercy. Yet when he was with us in Narnia, truly this Prince bore himself in another fashion than he does now in Tashbaan. For I take you all to witness what marvelous feats he did in that great tournament and hastilude

---

2. *The Horse and His Boy* (New York: Collier Books, 1970), 61.

which our brother the High King made for him, and how meekly and courteously he consorted with us the space of seven days. But here, in his own city, he has shown another face." (*The Horse and His Boy*, 61-62)

And when it became apparent that the Calormenes would not let them get away easily, she takes full responsibility for their dilemma: "'I am the cause of all this,' said Susan, bursting into tears. 'Oh, if only I had never left Cair Paravel. Our last happy day was before those ambassadors came from Calormen'" (*The Horse and His Boy*, 67).

In *Prince Caspian*, Lucy is the first one to see Aslan summoning them to go the opposite way. Susan maintained that Lucy was simply being naughty and headstrong, but when Aslan finally reveals himself to her, she puts everything right in exactly the right way.

"Lucy," said Susan in a very small voice.

"Yes?" said Lucy.

"I see him now. I'm sorry."

"That's all right."

"But I've been far worse than you know. I really believed it was him—he, I mean—yesterday. When he warned us not to go down to the fir wood. And I really believed it was him tonight, when you woke us up. I mean, deep down inside. Or I could have, if I'd let myself. But I just wanted to get out of the woods and—and—oh, I don't know. And what ever am I to say to him?"[3]

We are going to see in a moment that one of Susan's besetting temptations is that of anxiety and fear. Lewis elsewhere argues that certain vulnerabilities have corresponding strengths, and Susan's strength in this regard is tenderness. She is a great archer, but she is a great archer with a tender heart. When they rescue Trumpkin, it is through Susan's marksmanship:

> He floundered away to the far bank and Peter knew that Susan's arrow had struck his helmet. He turned and saw that she was very pale but was already fitting a second arrow to the string. But it was never used. (*Prince Caspian*, 29-30)

She did what she needed to do, but she didn't have to like it. She was "very pale." And when Edmund had a fencing match with Trumpkin, her response is plainly marked out: "Susan (who never could learn to like this sort of thing) shouted out, 'Oh, do be careful'" (*Prince Caspian*, 100).

And then it came to the archery contest between her and Trumpkin.

---

3. *Prince Caspian* (1951; New York: Collier Books, 1970), 147. All citations of this book are from this edition.

She was not enjoying her match half so much as Edmund had enjoyed his; not because she had any doubt about hitting the apple but because Susan was so tender-hearted that she almost hated to beat someone who had been beaten already. (*Prince Caspian*, 102)

And then, when she beats him, she tries to salvage Trumpkin's pride: "'It wasn't really any better than yours,' said Susan to the Dwarf. 'I think there was a tiny breath of wind as you shot'" (*Prince Caspian*, 102).

FEAR AND TIMIDITY

Throughout the stories, if someone is going to hang back, or regret having come, or be anxious about some new venture, that person is almost certainly Susan.

"I don't know that I'm going to like this place after all," said Susan. (*The Lion*, 55)

"I've a horrid feeling that Lu is right," said Susan. "I don't want to go a step further and I wish we'd never come." (*The Lion*, 56)

"Ooh!" said Susan, "I'd thought he was a man. Is he—quite safe? I shall feel rather nervous about meeting a lion." (*The Lion*, 75)

> "Then—have we no hope?" said Susan. (*The Lion*, 96)
>
> "How perfectly dreadful!" said Susan as they at last came back in despair. "Oh, how I wish we'd never come." (*The Lion*, 79)
>
> "Oh, do let's go back and go the other way," said Susan. "I knew all along we'd get lost in these woods." (*Prince Caspian*, 119)
>
> "Oh, do let's leave it alone," said Susan. "We can try it in the morning. If we've got to spend the night here I don't want an open door at my back and a great big black hole that anything might come out of, besides the draft and the damp." (*Prince Caspian*, 19-20)

That this is a feature of her personality, and not just something that affected her when she was an English schoolgirl in the strange land of Narnia, can be seen in how she responds at the very end of *The Lion, the Witch, and the Wardrobe*. She is a very great queen by this point, but she is still the one who urges them all to hang back: "'And in mine too,' said Queen Susan. 'Wherefore by my counsel we shall lightly return to our horses and follow this White Stag no further'" (*The Lion*, 184).

Lucy grows up into Lucy the Valiant, while Susan becomes Susan the Gentle:

"At Cair Paravel," said Corin. "She's not like Lucy, you know, who's as good as a man, or at any rate as good as a boy. Queen Susan is more like an ordinary grown-up lady. She doesn't ride to the wars." (*The Horse and His Boy*, 176)

Mark that comment that she is more like "an ordinary grown-up lady"—it will appear later.

After Susan apologized to Lucy in *Prince Caspian*, and said that she did not know what she would say to Aslan, what is actually notable is what Aslan said to her.

> Then, after an awful pause, the deep voice said, "Susan." Susan made no answer but the others thought she was crying. "You have listened to fears, child," said Aslan. "Come, let me breathe on you. Forget them. Are you brave again?"
> "A little, Aslan," said Susan. (*Prince Caspian*, 148)

Aslan is speaking here to the *center* of what troubled her—her tendency to listen to her fears.

THE BEAUTY OF SUSAN

Another standing issue in the books is the fact that Susan was regarded as the beauty, and Lucy not.

> Grown-ups thought her the pretty one of the family and she was no good at school work

(though otherwise very old for her age) and Mother said she "would get far more out of a trip to America than the youngsters." Edmund and Lucy tried not to grudge Susan her luck, but it was dreadful having to spend the summer holidays at their aunt's.[4]

Please note another aspect of this, which is that it was *the grown-ups* who thought her to be the beauty. She was flattered and reinforced in all of this, and it is not surprising that Lucy took this assessment on board also. This is why Lucy was tempted, in *The Voyage of the Dawn Treader*, to say a spell from the magician's book that would make her beautiful—over against Susan.

> Then it changed and Lucy, still beautiful beyond the lot of mortals, was back in England. And Susan (who had always been the beauty of the family) came home from America. The Susan in the picture looked exactly like the real Susan only plainer and with a nasty expression. And Susan was jealous of the dazzling beauty of Lucy, but that didn't matter a bit because no one cared anything about Susan now. (*The Voyage of the Dawn Treader*, 154)

---

4. *The Voyage of the Dawn Treader* (1952; New York: HarperTrophy, 1980), 5.

This was Lucy's temptation, not Susan's, but we should be able to connect the dots. All of these issues relate to one another. And that Susan was more beautiful actually, and not just in the opinion of the grown-ups, can be seen in Lewis's comment that when Lucy saw Aslan, she was almost as beautiful as she would have been had she uttered the spell. This tells us that Susan really was more beautiful, but Lucy wasn't plain.

GROWN-UP IN THE WRONG WAY

We have already seen that Susan was "old for her age," and so on. But Lewis has been giving us indications of this from the very beginning. At the start of their adventures in *Lion*, for example, Edmund is kicking against her grown-up-ness.

> "I think he's an old dear," said Susan.
>
> "Oh, come off it!" said Edmund, who was tired and pretending not to be tired, which always made him bad-tempered. "Don't go on talking like that."
>
> "Like what?" said Susan; "and anyway, it's time you were in bed."
>
> "Trying to talk like Mother," said Edmund. "And who are you to say when I'm to go to bed? Go to bed yourself." (*The Lion*, 2)

We see the same thing in *Prince Caspian*.

> "Where did you think you saw him?" asked Susan.
>
> "Don't talk like a grown-up," said Lucy, stamping her foot. "I didn't think I saw him. I saw him." (121)

When we are informed of Susan's absence from Aslan's country, this is the problem that is identified.

> "Sir," said Tirian, when he had greeted all these. "If I have read the chronicle aright, there should be another. Has not your Majesty two sisters? Where is Queen Susan?"
>
> "My sister Susan," answered Peter shortly and gravely, "is no longer a friend of Narnia."
>
> "Yes," said Eustace, "and whenever you've tried to get her to come and talk about Narnia or do anything about Narnia, she says 'What wonderful memories you have! Fancy your still thinking about all those funny games we used to play when we were children.'"[5]

In short, she had become a "grown-up" back in England, and this attitude is described as being "no longer a friend of Narnia."

> "Oh Susan!" said Jill. "She's interested in nothing nowadays except nylons and lipstick and in-

---

5. *The Last Battle* (1956; New York: Harper Collins, 2012), 154.

vitations. She always was a jolly sight too keen on being grown-up."

"Grown-up, indeed," said the Lady Polly. "I wish she would grow up. She wasted all her school time wanting to be the age she is now, and she'll waste all the rest of her life trying to stay that age. Her whole idea is to race on to the silliest time of one's life as quick as she can and then stop there as long as she can." (*The Last Battle*, 154)

It is not hard to connect this with the first set of temptations, her problems with her internal fears. We should have no difficulty imagining a beautiful girl who finds her identity in that beauty, and who has had that identity reinforced by all the grown-ups in her life. She is fearful of not getting there in time, and wants to hang onto it as long as she can once there. What is someone to do, if they find their identity in beauty, in a world where beauty fades?

But Aslan had known what Susan was returning to, and he had prepared her for it.

"Was that what Aslan was talking to you and Susan about this morning?" asked Lucy.

"Yes—that and other things," said Peter, his face very solemn. "I can't tell it all to you. There were things he wanted to say to Su and me because we're not coming back to Narnia." (*Prince Caspian*, 214)

In short, Aslan did not prepare her for what she would face back in England in order to abandon her there.

Now all this appeals to us, because nobody wants Susan to veer off into Aslan's shadow, never to be heard from again. But some might suspect that this is simply an emotional ploy on my part. Play the violins a little more sweetly—*surely* Aslan wouldn't do that to our friend Susan. But is there anything more substantive than this?

Yes.

CAIR PARAVEL OF THE FOUR THRONES

A strong doctrine of providence runs through all the Narnia stories. Aslan is behind everything. He pushed the boat with the infant Shasta in it ashore. He summons Eustace and Jill before they think to call on him. And when the four Pevensie children tumble into Narnia, they find *four* vacant thrones waiting for them. They are *destined* to rule at Cair Paravel. This is what drives the action of the story.

We are not told who built it, but the land of Narnia is *defined* by that great castle.

> "This is the land of Narnia," said the Faun, "where we are now; all that lies between the lamp-post and the great castle of Cair Paravel on the eastern sea. And you—you have come from the wild woods of the west?" (*The Lion*, 10)

When Tumnus confesses what he was about to do, he says something in passing about that great castle. The future of those four thrones was common knowledge—even if sometimes disbelieved.

> "And if she is extra and specially angry she'll turn me into stone and I shall be only a statue of a Faun in her horrible house until the four thrones at Cair Paravel are filled—and goodness knows when that will happen, or whether it will ever happen at all." (*The Lion*, 17)

We can also see the importance of the castle from the fact that the White Witch laid claim to it. She says she is the "Chatelaine of Cair Paravel, Empress" (*The Lion*, 55).

> "When Adam's flesh and Adam's bone
> Sits at Cair Paravel in throne,
> The evil time will be over and done." (*The Lion*, 76)

> "Because of another prophecy," said Mr. Beaver. "Down at Cair Paravel—that's the castle on the seacoast down at the mouth of this river which ought to be the capital of the whole country if all was as it should be—down at Cair Paravel there are four thrones and it's a saying in Narnia time out of mind that when two Sons of Adam and two Daughters of Eve sit on those four thrones, then

> it will be the end not only of the White Witch's reign but of her life, and that is why we had to be so cautious as we came along, for if she knew about you four, your lives wouldn't be worth a shake of my whiskers!" (*The Lion*, 78)

> "Why, all she wants is to get all four of you (she's thinking all the time of those four thrones at Cair Paravel)." (*The Lion*, 81)

> "Four thrones in Cair Paravel," said the Witch. "How if only three were filled? That would not fulfill the prophecy." (*The Lion*, 131)

The witch wanted to seize all four children in order to thwart the prophecy, but then realized, shortly before her attempt to kill Edmund, that *she could undo everything if only one of the four were missing*. In this case it was Edmund, but it would be equally true if it were Susan.

When Lucy and Susan were present at the resurrection of Aslan, it is not an insignificant detail that they were looking straight at Cair Paravel at the moment Aslan came back from the dead.

> Then at last, as they stood for a moment looking out toward the sea and Cair Paravel (which they could now just make out) the red turned to gold along the line where the sea and the sky

met and very slowly up came the edge of the sun. At that moment they heard from behind them a loud noise—a great cracking, deafening noise as if a giant had broken a giant's plate. (*The Lion*, 157-58)

His resurrection was to be the means of establishing those four children as kings and queens, and they were looking straight at their glorious future at the very moment he obtained it for them.

But perhaps the earlier "prophecies" were just loose Narnian chatter (you know how talking beasts are), or the anxious superstition of the witch. And Lucy and Susan facing toward the castle—well, they had to be facing *some* direction, didn't they? The real question is what Aslan thinks about Cair Paravel. So what does he call it?

"'That, O Man,' said Aslan, 'is Cair Paravel of the four thrones, in one of which you must sit as King. I show it to you because you are the firstborn and you will be High King over all the rest'" (*The Lion*, 126).

Aslan himself calls it "Cair Paravel *of the four thrones*." I would submit to you that to have one of the four thrones of Cair Paravel sitting permanently empty is not really a literary possibility.

> The castle of Cair Paravel on its little hill towered up above them; before them were the sands, with rocks and little pools of salt water,

and seaweed, and the smell of the sea and long miles of bluish-green waves breaking for ever and ever on the beach. And oh, the cry of the seagulls! Have you heard it? Can you remember? (*The Lion*, 178)

This is why Aslan gave the four of them a solemn promise. And it was a promise, grounded in the will of the Emperor-over-the-sea.

"'Once a king or queen in Narnia, *always a king or queen*. Bear it well, Sons of Adam! Bear it well, Daughters of Eve!' said Aslan" (*The Lion*, 179, emphasis mine).

Once a queen, always a queen. Bear it well, *daughters*.

WHAT DO THEY TEACH THEM IN THESE SCHOOLS?

All this should be sufficient, but I would like to cinch it just a little bit tighter.

Lewis was a Christian Platonist, but he does this in a really admirable way. He turns Plato on his head. Platonism held that the realm of the Forms represented ultimate reality, and that this world was a dim reflection of that ultimate reality. But for Plato, the realm of the Forms would not have been material, tangible, or dense with molecules. Rather, Plato was thinking of an upscale Euclidville. His was a rationalistic and philosophical project.

Lewis—plainly in both *The Last Battle* and *The Great Divorce,* and subtly in *Letters to Malcolm*—inverts all this, and makes the realm of the Forms denser and more real than our vapory world down here.

They found themselves in the new Narnia, in the real Narnia. And this Narnia was *more* solid, not more "spiritual."

> "Kings and Queens," he cried, "we have all been blind. We are only beginning to see where we are. From up there I have seen it all—Ettinsmuir, Beaversdam, the Great River, *and Cair Paravel* still shining on the edge of the Eastern Sea. Narnia is not dead. This is Narnia." (*The Last Battle*, 194, emphasis mine)

When the eagle flew up to see all this, he saw everything that mattered, and that included Cair Paravel. And Cair Paravel in the heavenly Narnia would still be Cair Paravel of the four thrones.

> "It was only a shadow or a copy of the real Narnia which has always been here and always will be here: just as our own world, England and all, is only a shadow or copy of something in Aslan's real world. You need not mourn over Narnia, Lucy. All of the old Narnia that mattered, all the dear creatures, have been drawn into the real Narnia through the Door." (*The Last Battle*, 195)

All of the old Narnia that mattered. That would include Susan's throne, would it not?

Not only so, but Lewis postulates an inverted Russian doll cosmos, with each internal world being bigger and more material than the world which encased it. So when they go "further up and further in," they come eventually to the *real* garden that was behind the shadow garden where Digory got the apple. Another world would be inside *that* garden, and that third world is yet another Narnia. And as they gaze at this backwards onion, where each layer is greater than the one before, what do they see?

> "Of course, Daughter of Eve," said the Faun. "The further up and the further in you go, the bigger everything gets. The inside is larger than the outside." Lucy looked hard at the garden and saw that it was not really a garden but a whole world, with its own rivers and woods and sea and mountains. But they were not strange: she knew them all.
>
> "I see," she said. "This is still Narnia, and more real and more beautiful than the Narnia down below, just as it was more real and more beautiful than the Narnia outside the stable door! I see . . . world within world, Narnia within Narnia. . . ."
>
> "Yes," said Mr. Tumnus, "like an onion: except that as you continue to go in and in, each circle is larger than the last." (*The Last Battle*, 207)

"She could see the whole Southern desert and beyond it the great city of Tashbaan: to Eastward *she could see Cair Paravel on the edge of the sea* and the very window of the room that had once been her own." (*The Last Battle*, 207, emphasis mine)

Of *course* she could see Cair Paravel. Was it still Cair Paravel of the four thrones? When she could see the very window of the room that had been hers, I wonder if she could see Susan's room, too. Not to put too fine a point on it, I refuse to believe that a craftsman like Lewis would have the shadow Cair Paravel be Cair Paravel of the four thrones, and the second and third Cair Paravels to be limited to three. Not possible.

So when they get into the third Narnia, much greater and larger than the first two, it is here that they can start to see the joining of all worlds. It is here that they see the real England, where their parents are, who are soon to join them.

So we need to be careful. The shadowland Narnia has gone through its final judgment. All of the first Narnia is either here in the third Narnia, or they had veered off into Aslan's shadow. That was not the case with England. The Pevensie parents were there because of a train accident, and not because of the Eschaton in our world. Susan was not with them because Susan was still alive, in England. In fact, she is probably *still* there, a nice old lady in her nineties, somewhere in Oxfordshire.

IN SUM

I would have been prepared to cheerfully grant difficulties for my thesis if Susan had been traveling with her parents by train, and if she had died in the train wreck together with them, and had then not shown up in the real Narnia, the Narnia beyond. That would be a real difficulty. It is hard to maintain that someone is in Heaven when, as all can plainly see, she's not there.

But the Susan of this story is the surviving Pevensie, if you can call life in the shadowlands surviving. Her parents had died. Her brothers and sisters had died. She was left alone, and her story was not close to being done. We can rest assured that she would come at the last to her rightful place, and be seated on one of the four great thrones in the ultimate Cair Paravel. And if we inquired *too* closely into what would need to have happened to her in order to bring all this about, we can be assured that this would be a sure way to get Aslan to growl at us.

But what would C.S. Lewis himself think about an argument like this one? He was characteristically coy about things like this, but I do think he would have concurred with it. At the very least, he would certainly grant the possibility. As he wrote to one young correspondent:

The books don't tell us what happened to Susan. She is left alive in this world at the end, having by then turned into a rather silly, conceited young woman. But there is plenty of time for her to mend, and perhaps she will get to Aslan's country in the end—in her own way. I think that whatever she had seen in Narnia she *could* (if she was the sort that wanted to) persuade herself, as she grew up, that it was "all nonsense."[6]

Once a queen in Narnia, always a queen in Narnia.

---

6. *The Collected Letters of C. S. Lewis, Vol. 3: Narnia, Cambridge, and Joy 1950-1963*, ed. Walter Hooper (New York: Harper Collins, 2007), 826 [letter to Martin Kilmer, January 22, 1957].

CHAPTER 3
THE CURIOUS PRESENCE OF EMETH

One episode in the Narnia stories has caused no little consternation for evangelical parents as they have read to their children, and that element of the story concerns the salvation of Emeth. In the previous chapter, I discussed the curious fact of Susan's absence from the heavenly regions in *The Last Battle*. A second curious fact has to do with Emeth's *presence* there, and with Lewis's reasons for including him.

As we consider this, it is important to get one particular distinction out of the way at the outset. In the minds of many evangelical believers, a "broad inclusion" of non-Christians in the heavenly kingdom is indistinguishable from theological liberalism. And with regard to an ecumenical "comparative religions" approach, this instinct is quite correct. "We are all seeking after God, each in our own way" is a central aspect of the theological left, and as such must be rejected by all faithful Christians. The problem with that approach is—as the apostle Paul might put it—that a religion of God-seekers is an empty set. No one seeks after God (Rom. 3:11).

If this broad and inclusive approach were true, then Christ died for nothing. With a sorrow deeper than any man has ever experienced, Christ asked His Father to have the cup pass from Him if there were any other way (Matt. 26:39). If the Father could have said something like, "Well, the *Rig Veda* has some promising developments," then why did Jesus have to die? Jesus had to die because there was no other way to save us.

The purpose of this essay is to take the salvation of Emeth as a starting point for a discussion of "who then can be saved?"—with that discussion occurring among conservative believers who accept the authority of Scripture, and the uniqueness and sufficiency of Christ.

While it is quite true that Lewis shows more latitude on this question than the average conservative believer does, that difference of opinion we have with him is not in the same category as the difference we would have with a theological liberal. More is going on with Lewis, as I hope to show. Lewis says this:

But the truth is God has not told us what His arrangement about the other people are. We do know that no man can be saved except through Christ; we do not know that only those who know Him can be saved through Him.[1]

There is something to differ with here, surely. But it should be plain that this is not a position that says "we are all saying the same thing really."

In other words, it *is* liberalism to say that faithful Muslims, or Buddhists, or Hindus, each following the tenets of their own religion sincerely, can be saved for being good people. This is pernicious and false. It is quite a separate question to ask whether God in His sovereignty can reach down into a filthy religion, like the worship of Tash, and do an extraordinary thing by saving someone from all of that. In such a case, that person is not saved *by means of* his religion, whatever he conceives it to be, but rather is saved *from* that religion, by grace through faith.

THE CASE OF EMETH

I won't do a great deal of explaining the context of the following citations, assuming as I am that the reader of a book like this one is also a close reader of things Narnian. I am assuming you know the story,

---

1. *Mere Christianity* (1952; New York: Macmillan, 1984), 65.

and will only place a few reminders here and there. The Calormenes are running a scam at the Stable, with Shift the ape as their tool. Narnians are being invited by Rishda Tarkaan to go into the Stable to view "Aslan," and to everyone's surprise, Emeth volunteers to go in.

> "Nay, my Father," answered Emeth. "Thou hast said that their Aslan and our Tash are all one. And if that is the truth, then Tash himself is in yonder. And how then sayest thou that I have nothing to do with him? For gladly would I die a thousand deaths if I might look once on the face of Tash."
>
> "Thou art a fool and understandest nothing," said Rishda Tarkaan. "These be high matters."
>
> Emeth's face grew sterner. "Is it then not true that Tash and Aslan are all one?" he asked. "Has the Ape lied to us?"
>
> "Of course they're all one," said the Ape.
>
> "Swear it, Ape," said Emeth.
>
> "Oh dear!" whimpered Shift, "I wish you'd all stop bothering me. My head does ache. Yes, yes, I swear it."
>
> "Then, my Father," said Emeth, "I am utterly determined to go in." (*The Last Battle*, 126)

Emeth despises the lies and hypocrisy that he sees as characteristic of the Calormene venture into

Narnia. He is a devotee of his god, entirely sold out to Tash, but in a way that places him entirely at odds with the wickedness of that religion, and with the behavior of all his compatriots.

> Emeth came walking forward into the open strip of grass between the bonfire and the stable. His eyes were shining, his face very solemn, his hand was on his sword-hilt, and he carried his head high. Jill felt like crying when she looked at his face. And Jewel whispered in the King's ear, "By the Lion's Mane, I almost love this young warrior, Calormene though he be. He is worthy of a better god than Tash." (*The Last Battle*, 127)

The Narnians, watching him approach the Stable, feel an immediate affinity with him. And the thing they see—which Emeth does not yet see—is how he is utterly at odds with his own religion. He is worthy of a better god than that.

After the fighting is all over, and the old world has ended, and the saved are sorting things out in the new Narnia, the party of Narnians comes across Emeth who, when he entered the Stable, had found himself in Aslan's country.

> The others followed where the Dogs led them and found a young Calormene sitting under a

chestnut tree beside a clear stream of water. It was Emeth. He rose at once and bowed gravely.

"Sir," he said to Peter, "I know not whether you are my friend or my foe, but I should count it my honor to have you for either. Has not one of the poets said that a noble friend is the best gift and a noble enemy the next best?"

"Sir," said Peter, "I do not know that there need be any war between you and us." (*The Last Battle*, 183-84)

When they ask him to tell his story, they find out just how remarkable it was. Emeth had yearned to go to war with Narnia, in honest, open battle, but when the actual plan was revealed, he was distraught.

"And most of all when I found we must wait upon a Monkey, and when it began to be said that Tash and Aslan were one, then the world became dark in my eyes. For always since I was a boy I have served Tash and my great desire was to know more of him, if it might be, to look upon his face. But the name of Aslan was hateful to me." (*The Last Battle*, 185-86)

After Emeth found himself in the heavenly country, he had an encounter with Aslan. And the astonishing thing is that Aslan welcomed him.

"Then I fell at his feet and thought, Surely this is the hour of death, for the Lion (who is worthy of all honor) will know that I have served Tash all my days and not him. Nevertheless, it is better to see the Lion and die than to be Tisroc of the world and live and not to have seen him. But the Glorious One bent down his golden head and touched my forehead with his tongue and said, *Son, thou art welcome.*" (*The Last Battle*, 188, emphasis added)

In the subsequent interaction, they get into the theology of the thing, which is where things get interesting.

"But I said, Alas, Lord, I am no son of thine but the servant of Tash. He answered, Child, all the service thou hast done to Tash, I account as service done to me. Then by reasons of my great desire for wisdom and understanding, I overcame my fear and questioned the Glorious One and said, Lord, is it then true, as the Ape said, that thou and Tash are one? The Lion growled so that the earth shook (but his wrath was not against me) and said, It is false." (*The Last Battle*, 188-89)

So whatever else Lewis is saying, he is not saying that Aslan and Tash are one, or that all religions teach the same thing, or that we all ascend by different paths up the same mountain.

> "Not because he and I are one, but because we are opposites, I take to me the services which thou hast done to him. For I and he are of such different kinds that no service which is vile can be done to me, and none which is not vile can be done to him." (*The Last Battle*, 189)

This is not the comparative religion, Coexist-bumper-sticker approach. Tash is a foul god, like Molech in the Old Testament. God saves sinners, and He saves them *out of* brothels, taverns, casinos, and temples of Tash.

Now half of what Lewis says here is a commonplace among evangelical believers. It is self-evidently true that hypocrites who offer vile behavior to the true God are actually worshiping a false god, and rendering what they are actually offering in another direction entirely. This is preeminently a biblical concept.

On one occasion, Jesus was speaking to pious Jews who had believed in Him (John 8:31), and He wound up saying this:

> "Ye are of *your father the devil*, and the lusts of your father ye will do." (John 8:44a, emphasis added)

> "They shall put you out of the synagogues: yea, the time cometh, that whosoever killeth you *will think that he doeth God service*." (John 16:2, emphasis added)

So it is true that someone who claims to be serving Aslan, but who is doing vile things, is actually serving Tash. That's the easy one.

But can it go the other way? Can someone claim to be serving Tash, like Emeth, and actually be serving Aslan? Something of a reverse hypocrite? Someone in a foul religion being fair, living in a way contrary to what that the religion requires? Emeth had been going in the "wrong" direction, as far as Tash was concerned, since he was a boy. As far as Tash was concerned, Emeth had been a heretic for a long time.

Lewis puts it this way.

> "Therefore if any man swear by Tash and keep his oath for the oath's sake, it is by me that he has truly sworn, though he know it not, and it is I who reward him. And if any man do a cruelty in my name, then, though he says the name Aslan, it is Tash whom he serves and by Tash his deed is accepted. Dost thou understand, Child? I said, Lord, thou knowest how much I understand."
> (*The Last Battle*, 189)

So taking all this at face value, this was salvation *from* the religion of Tash—by extraordinary means—not salvation by means of the religion of Tash. Emeth was not the fulfillment of that religion, he was delivered out of it, just as Aravis was delivered out of it.

And incidentally, I should mention in passing that the entire culture of the Calormenes is obviously a stand-in for Islam. This is most explicit at the beginning of chapter 4 of *The Horse and His Boy* when Lewis describes Tashbaan as having numerous minarets—and a minaret is a tower attached to a mosque.

> "But I said also (for the truth constrained me), Yet I have been seeking Tash all my days. Beloved, said the Glorious One, unless thy desire had been for me thou wouldst not have sought so long and so truly. For all find what they truly seek. Then he breathed upon me and took away the trembling from my limbs and caused me to stand upon my feet. And after that, he said not much but that we should meet again, and I must go further up and further in. Then he turned him about in a storm and flurry of gold and was gone suddenly." (*The Last Battle*, 189)

Emeth sought for what he did both "long" and "truly," but this was Aslan's doing in him, and for him. It was not the doing of Tash. It was Emeth being led, by extraordinary means, away from Tash.

So that leads naturally to the question whether such extraordinary interventions actually occur. Does God ever bypass the ordinary means of preaching the gospel in order to save people from their bondage in pagan religions?

SO WHAT IS PAGANISM?

We have several difficulties to sort out simultaneously. The first one is that Narnia doesn't really have a new covenant era and an old covenant era. Aslan dies and rises in the midst of Narnian history, but there is nothing corresponding to the Old Testament history of the Jews being supplanted by the New Testament structure of the church. The second difficulty is that Gentiles in the Old Testament were not synonymous with unbelievers in the New. Most of them were unbelievers, but it was possible to be a Gentile and a devout believer.

This matters because in the Old Testament the relationship between the Jews and the Gentiles was NOT comparable to the relationship between Christians and non-Christians today.

In the fourth chapter of Acts, the apostles did a great miracle and were challenged on it. By what power or *name* have you done this (Acts 4:7)? They responded that this man stands before you whole by the *name* of Jesus Christ of Nazareth (Acts 4:10). And this led to the great confession:

"Neither is there salvation in any other: for there is none other name under heaven given among men, whereby we must be saved" (Acts 4:12).

The necessity of preaching the gospel to every creature today can be seen in this. Nonbelievers are not brought to salvation through the power of an anonymous Christ, working behind the scenes.

They are saved through the preaching of the *name*. And if they want to be saved, they must themselves call upon the name. The priesthood of believers has been expanded to all the nations of men, which is why all men are summoned to believe and be baptized.

"And such were some of you: but ye are washed, but ye are sanctified, but ye are justified *in the name of the Lord Jesus*, and by the Spirit of our God" (1 Cor. 6:11, emphasis added).

In short, nonbelievers who want to be saved today have an obligation today to repent and believe, calling upon the name of Jesus. Non-Christians have a moral obligation to become Christians.

In the course of his Mars Hill address, about which more in a little bit, Paul says this:

"And the times of this ignorance God winked at; but now commandeth all men everywhere to repent" (Acts 17:30).

We see here that the command to repent, given to all men, is not negotiable. The Christian faith is one of world conquest. Everyone must repent, and everyone must believe (Matt. 28:18-20). It is an authoritative summons. But in the same verse, we are also told that the previous ignorance of pagan nations, prior to the coming of Christ, was something that God "winked at." The word there literally means *overlooked*. God *disregarded* it.

Huh.

So in the Old Testament, Gentiles were under no obligation whatever to become Jews. They could be saved without becoming Jews, and many of them were saved without becoming Jews. The Jews were not the believers of the Old Testament, but were rather the priestly people of the Old Testament. They served in this function *for the sake of* the Gentile nations.

Melchizedek was not a Jew, but he was a priest of the Most High God, and the father of all the Jews paid the tithe to him (Gen. 14:18). Jethro, priest of Midian (Exod. 3:1), the father-in-law of Moses, was not a Jew, and yet was a worshiper of the true God. Balaam was an ungodly man, but was apparently a genuine prophet, with the genuine prophetic gift (Num. 22:9). Naaman the Syrian became a worshiper of the true God, and the prophet gave him standing permission to continue to push his master's wheelchair into the House of Rimmon (2 Kings 5:18). And let us not forget the massive revival in Nineveh that was brought about through the preaching of Jonah (Matt. 12:41).

When Solomon built the Temple, the structure included a way for Gentiles, pagans, to pray to the true and living God—while remaining Gentiles. The language is quite striking.

> Moreover concerning the stranger, *which is not of thy people Israel*, but is come from a far country for thy great name's sake, and thy mighty hand,

and thy stretched out arm; if they come and pray in this house; *Then hear thou from the heavens, even from thy dwelling place, and do according to all that the stranger calleth to thee for*; that all people of the earth may know thy name, and fear thee, as doth thy people Israel, and may know that this house which I have built is called by thy name. (2 Chron. 6:32–33, emphasis added)

When Jesus cleanses the Temple, He drives out the merchants and moneychangers *from the Court of the Gentiles.* The Gentiles had a court at the Temple, designated for them to worship the true God, and without becoming Jews first. The clean sacrificial animals represented the Jews, and they had filled up the place that had been reserved for the Gentiles. This is why Jesus' rebuke was a two-edged rebuke. They had filled the Temple with their thieveries, and they had excluded the Gentiles by means of it.

"And he taught, saying unto them, Is it not written, My house shall be called *of all nations* the house of prayer? but ye have made it a den of thieves" (Mark 11:17, emphasis added).

The Temple in Jerusalem was for all the Gentiles. Were there any Emeths among them? And keep in mind that even though we don't have an old covenant/new covenant distinction, a great deal of the Narnian context does have a B.C. feel to it. For example, centaurs prophesying is not something that frequently happened in the post-apostolic period.

The apostle Paul calls the Cretan Epimenides a *prophet*—a "prophet, one of their own" (Tit. 1:12-13). And when he is preaching at Mars Hill, he takes as his starting point the altar to the unknown god. Whose idea was *that* kind of altar? Well, it turns out that the idea came from this same Epimenides, who had been summoned from Crete centuries before by the leaders of Athens in order to deal with a plague that was afflicting the city at that time. Epimenides dealt with it, in part, by having them establish altars to the unknown god, which they did, stopping the plague. Later Paul starts with one of those altars as his text, and in the course of his preaching, he quotes Epimenides directly: "For in him we live, and move, and have our being; as certain also of your own poets have said, For we are also his offspring" (Acts 17:28).

Live, move and have our being is from Epimenides. The second citation, *for we are also his offspring* is from a gent named Aratus. The thing that is interesting about that quotation is that it is from a hymn to *Zeus*. Not Tash, Zeus. And the thing we must understand is that there was the celebrity Zeus, the Zeus of legend, the Zeus who was entirely unaffected by the #MeToo movement, the Zeus who was an embarrassment to thoughtful pagans. And then there was the Zeus as Emeth and Aratus conceived him to be. This does not make their conceptions orthodox—remember that Paul is about to say that God *overlooked* much ignorance. He did not overlook overt evil, as the destruction of Sodom showed, but He overlooked a great deal.

REFORMED CAUTION

Just a few more comments in closing. The father of the modern evangelical hesitancy to allow for any true salvation outside of a plain proclamation of the death and resurrection of Jesus Christ may well have been Martin Luther. He was a theologian of the cross, and if the cross was not preached to you, well, then, too bad for you. This contrasts sharply with the attitude of Zwingli, who was happy to kick open the gates of Paradise to the likes of Socrates and Hercules.

The ancient phrase captures our question in a nutshell. *Extra ecclesiam nulla salus*—outside the church there is no salvation. Is that true, and how strict should we be with it? But oddities and quirks can occur to our minds almost right away. What about the guy who is hit by a car on the way to his baptism?

The Westminster Confession, to which I subscribe, has in my view a balanced and nicely nuanced approach to the problem.

> The visible Church, which is also catholic or universal under the Gospel (not confined to one na-

tion, as before under the law), consists of all those throughout the world that profess the true religion; and of their children: and is the kingdom of the Lord Jesus Christ, the house and family of God, out of which there is *no ordinary possibility* of salvation. (WCF 25.2, emphasis added)

Elect infants, dying in infancy, are regenerated, and saved by Christ, through the Spirit, who works when, and where, and how he pleases: so also are all other elect persons who are *incapable of being outwardly called* by the ministry of the Word. (WCF 10.3, emphasis added)

The grace of faith, whereby the elect are enabled to believe to the saving of their souls, is the work of the Spirit of Christ in their hearts, and is *ordinarily wrought* by the ministry of the Word, by which also, and by the administration of the sacraments, and prayer, it is increased and strengthened. (WCF 14.1, emphasis added)

Must someone be called by the explicit preaching of the Word, and be baptized and brought into the visible church in order to be saved? Their answer is "usually." The named exceptions that they point to are elect infants dying in infancy, and other incapacitated individuals (e.g. the severely retarded) who cannot respond to the preaching of the Word in the ordinary way. God's elective decree can touch them there.

And we also know that in the old covenant, God's elective decree could touch the elect among the Hittites and Assyrians also. Does this change in the new covenant? I would argue that it does gradually and inexorably change as the gospel makes its progress through the world. The more the gospel spreads, the less possible it is for any kind of ignorance to be overlooked, and such "winking" was rare to begin with.

But if a centurion just like Cornelius were living in the westernmost part of the empire a century later, what would his status be? The question is not easy for us to answer, which is fortunate, because the disposal of all such situations is not in our hands, but rather in God's.

So then, back to Emeth. If you visualize him as the devout Muslim who refuses to respond to the gospel, and who insists on attending his mosque instead, the scenario in *The Last Battle* really is problematic. But if you visualize him as someone in the position of Naaman the Syrian, the problem becomes much less acute.

CHAPTER 4
THE LIGHT FROM BEHIND THE SUN

Many years ago, one of the first books I wrote was published under the name *Persuasions*, and the subtitle was "A Dream of Reason Meeting Unbelief." In that book, a character named Evangelist encountered various people on the road that leads to the Abyss and he engaged them in conversation, seeking to persuade them to turn and head in the other direction.

Now these were the pre-Cambrian days before the internet, and theological book junkies like myself used to rely on monthly newsprint catalogs that would get the word out about books that might interest all the junkies out there. One of these fine publications was called Great Christian Books, and so we sent on a copy of my book to them in the hopes that they would include it as one of their titles. They agreed to do so, which was a really big deal for me at the time. When I got my copy of that month's catalog, I eagerly looked up my book, and discovered that the good folks at Great Christian Books had written the copy for it. It read something like: "This small book is a fine introduction to Van Tillian apologetics . . . ." I stared at that with something akin to consternation, and thought something like, "It *is*?"

I had heard of Van Til, but had not read him. So what was I doing running around writing little introductions to his apologetic approach? In haste I ordered a copy of *The Defense of the Faith*, probably from Great Christian Books, and breathed a sigh of relief after I read it. I guess I was Van Tillian. There are worse things, I suppose.

But where had I learned it? The element in my book that caused GCB to tag me as a Van Tillian was a method of argumentation that I had learned from C.S. Lewis, most probably from his book *Miracles*. This was odd, because there is a section in *The Defense of the Faith* where Van Til was quite critical of Lewis. And this in turn was understandable because there *are* a number of places where Lewis does in fact reason like an evidentialist, and reasoning like an evidentialist gave Van Till the jim jams. But there is also a great theme running through his work—his argument from reason—that I would regard as a high-octane presuppositional approach.

And this line of argument is not at all incidental to his thought, as I would like to show here. I learned to think this way from Lewis, and I want show homage here.

Because of this central theme in Lewis's thought, I think it is fair to say that his use of evidences is closer to what Greg Bahnsen described as "debris clearing" than it is to a "neutralist" evidentialist approach. That's as may be, and you all can evaluate my reasons for thinking this below.

THE ANSCOMBE EPISODE

This argument from reason that Lewis advances is best known from his book *Miracles*, in the third chapter of which Lewis set out the self-contradiction of naturalism. His particular formulation of this argument was challenged at a meeting of the Socratic Club at Oxford by the philosopher Elizabeth Anscombe, and the two debated it there. As a result of that interaction, Lewis adjusted the wording of his argument in subsequent editions of *Miracles*, clarifying what he meant, and sharpening his argument. In my view, whatever form the argument takes—although this may be just me—it is a slam-dunk, knock-down, set-the-tattered-remains-on-fire argument.

But as a result of Lewis making these adjustments in response to Anscombe, a myth has grown up in unbelieving circles that says that the great "apologist" Lewis got his clock cleaned by a *real* philosopher, and as a consequence he retired from the field of apologetics and took to writing about fauns, centaurs, and talking lions. Whatever Narnia has going for it, the jibe might go, we have to include the fact that there are no real philosophers there who might burst the bubble of your apologetic method.

Those who want to read further about the background of the Anscombe/Lewis debate, and the actual details of it, should check out *C.S. Lewis's Dangerous Idea* by Victor Reppert. My purpose here is not to go over the same territory that Reppert covers, but rather simply to show how Lewis did not back away from this argument in the slightest, as established by a glance at his overall time line. This argument was at the center of how Lewis became a Christian in the first place, and he advanced it over and over again, clean through to the end of his life.

THE ARGUMENT IN BRIEF

A blind, purposeless, and material process does not and cannot know that it is blind, or purposeless, or material. It cannot know anything. If thought is simply the froth on the waves of our brain activity, then one of the first things that thought loses is the ability to know that there is even such a *thing* as brain activity, or froth for that matter. If human argumentation is simply the epiphenomena that our brain chemistry produces, then there is absolutely no reason to trust human argumentation—including any arguments that urge us to believe that argumentation is simply the epiphenomena that our brain chemistry produces. If reason is simply what these chemicals do under these conditions and at this temperature, then we cannot even know that such things as "chemicals" exist, and we certainly cannot know about "conditions" and "temperatures."

In short, we need not do battle with materialistic atheism. They do show up to the fight but before any swords are out, the foe draws a dagger and cuts his own throat.

And far from backing away from this line of argument, C.S. Lewis made this argument the theme of his life's work in apologetics. Taking slightly different forms, it shows up again and again and again. In the citations I have collected below, I have sought to arrange them (roughly) in chronological order. There will be a lot of quotations, so please bear with me. I will make just a few comments as we go along, and will make myself free to italicize within Lewis's quotations for emphasis.

THE CITATIONS

Although *Surprised by Joy* was written later in his life, Lewis was describing how he first became a Christian. And this is part of what he said:

> We maintained that abstract thought (if obedient to logical rules) gave indisputable truth . . . .

Barfield convinced me that it was inconsistent. If thought were a purely subjective event, these claims for it would have to be abandoned. If one kept (as rock-bottom reality) the universe of the senses, aided by instruments and co-ordinated so as to form "science," then one would have to go much further—as many have since gone—and adopt a Behaviorist's theory of logic, ethics, and aesthetics. But such a theory was, and is, unbelievable to me. I am using the word "unbelievable," which many use to mean "improbably" or even "undesirable," in a quite literal sense. *I mean that the act of believing what the behaviorist believes is one that my mind simply will not perform.* I cannot force my thought into that shape any more than I can scratch my ear with my big toe or pour wine out of a bottle into the cavity at the base of that same bottle.[1]

In short, if thought is subjective, there is no reason to trust my thought that thought is subjective. There was a reason why Lewis could not bend his mind into that particular shape—it *wasn't* a shape. It was inchoate nonsense.

After his conversion, the first book Lewis published was *The Pilgrim's Regress*. As an allegory about many of the intellectual follies of that era, it

---

1. *Surprised by Joy* (New York: Harvest/HBJ Book, 1956), 208-209, emphasis added.

is not surprising that this argument appears there. This book was published in 1933, and in this place Reason is speaking.

> "The Spirit of the Age wishes to allow argument and not to allow argument."
>
> "How is that?"
>
> "You heard what they said. If anyone argues with them they say that he is rationalizing his own desires, and therefore need not be answered. But if anyone listens to them they will then argue themselves to show that their own doctrines are true."
>
> "I see. And what is the cure for this?"
>
> "*You must ask them whether any reasoning is valid or not.* If they say no, then their own doctrines, being reached by reasoning, fall to the ground. If they say yes, then they will have to examine your arguments and refute them on their merits: for if some reasoning is valid, for all they know, your bit of reasoning may be one of the valid bits."[2]

In 1941, Lewis says this in an interaction with a Dr. Joad: "I agree with Dr. Joad in rejecting mechanism and emergent evolution. Mechanism, like all materialist systems, breaks down at the problem of knowledge.

---

2. *The Pilgrim's Regress: An Allegorical Apology for Christianity, Reason, and Romanticism* (1933; Grand Rapids: William B. Eerdmans, 1995), 63, emphasis added.

> *If thought is the undesigned and irrelevant product of cerebral motions, what reason have we to trust it?*"[3]

Sometime during the Second World War, Lewis wrote this:

> There is therefore no question of a total scepticism about human thought. We are always prevented from accepting total scepticism because it can be formulated only by making a tacit exception in favour of the thought we are thinking at the moment—just as the man who warns the newcomer "Don't trust anyone in this office" always expects you to trust him at that moment . . . . *It therefore follows that all knowledge whatever depends on the validity of inference.* If, in principle, the feeling of certainty we have when we say "Because A is B therefore C must be D" is an illusion, if it reveals only how our cortex has to work and not how realities external to us must really be, *then we can know nothing whatever.*[4]

Lewis said this in 1942:

> The belief in such a supernatural reality itself can neither be proved nor disproved by experi-

---

3. C.S. Lewis, "Evil and God," in *C.S. Lewis Essay Collection*, 93, emphasis added.

4. "De Futilitate," in *Christian Reflections* (1967; Grand Rapids: William B. Eerdmans, 1977), 61, 62-63, emphasis added.

ence. The arguments for its existence are metaphysical, *and to me conclusive*. They turn on the fact that even to think and act in the natural world we have to assume something beyond it and even assume that we partly belong to that something. *In order to think we must claim for our own reasoning a validity which is not credible if our own thought is merely a function of our brain, and our brains a by-product of irrational physical processes.* In order to act, above the level of mere impulse, we must claim a similar validity for our judgments of good and evil. In both cases we get the same disquieting result. The concept of nature itself is one we have reached only tacitly by claiming a sort of *super*-natural status for ourselves.[5]

In *Mere Christianity* (1943), Lewis reasons in the same way.

> My argument against God was that the universe seemed so cruel and unjust. But how had I got this idea of *just* and *unjust*? A man does not call a line crooked unless he has some idea of a straight line. What was I comparing this universe with when I called it unjust? If the whole show was bad and senseless from A to Z, so to speak, why

---

5. "Miracles" in *God in the Dock: Essays in Theology and Ethics*, ed. Walter Hooper (Grand Rapids: William B. Eerdmans, 1970), 27, emphasis added.

did I, who was supposed to be part of the show, find myself in such violent reaction against it? A man feels wet when he falls into water, because man is not a water animal: a fish would not feel wet. Of course I could have given up my idea of justice by saying it was nothing but a private idea of my own. But if I did that, then my argument against God collapsed too—for the argument depended on saying that the world was really unjust, not simply that it did not happen to please my fancies. *Thus in the very act of trying to prove that God did not exist—in other words, that the whole of reality was senseless—I found I was forced to assume that one part of reality—namely my idea of justice—was full of sense.* Consequently atheism turns out to be too simple. If the whole universe has no meaning, we should never have found out that it has no meaning: just as, if there were no light in the universe and therefore no creatures with eyes, we should never know it was dark. *Dark* would be a word without meaning. (*Mere Christianity*, 45-46, emphasis added)

Then in 1944, Lewis wrote this:

If the solar system was brought about by an accidental collision, then the appearance of organic life on this planet was also an accident, and the whole evolution of Man was an accident too. If so, then all our present thoughts are mere accidents—the accidental by-product of the movement of atoms. And this holds for the thoughts of the materialists and astronomers as well as for anyone else's. But if *their* thoughts—i.e. of Materialism and Astronomy—are merely accidental by-products, why should we believe them to be true? I see no reason for believing that one accident should be able to give me a correct account of all the other accidents. *It's like expecting that the accidental shape taken by the splash when you upset a milk-jug should give you a correct account of how the jug was made and why it was upset.*[6]

The book *Miracles* was published in 1947, and in the original form, it was this that drew criticism from Elizabeth Anscombe.

> All possible knowledge, then, depends on the validity of reasoning. If the feeling of certainty which we express by words like *must be* and *therefore* and *since* is a real perception of how things outside our own minds really "must" be, well and good. But if this certainty is merely a feeling *in* our own minds and not a genuine insight into realities beyond them—if it merely represents the way our minds happen to work—then we can

---

6. "Answers to Questions on Christianity," in *God in the Dock*, 52-53; emphasis added.

have no knowledge. Unless human reasoning is valid no science can be true.

It follows that no account of the universe can be true unless that account leaves it possible for our thinking to be a real insight. A theory which explained everything else in the whole universe but which made it impossible to believe that our thinking was valid, would be utterly out of court. For that theory would itself have been reached by thinking, and if thinking is not valid that theory would, of course, be itself demolished. It would have destroyed its own credentials. *It would be an argument which proved that no argument was sound—a proof that there are no such things as proofs—which is nonsense.*

Thus a strict materialism refutes itself for the reason given long ago by Professor Haldane: "If my mental processes are determined wholly by the motions of atoms in my brain, I have no reason to suppose that my beliefs are true . . . and hence I have no reason for supposing my brain to be composed of atoms." (*Possible Worlds*, p. 209)[7]

Lewis says the same thing again, a year later, in 1948.

Whenever you know what the other man is saying is wholly due to his complexes or to a bit of

---

7. *Miracles: A Preliminary Study* (1947; New York: Harper Collins, 2002), rev. ed., 21–22, emphasis added.

bone pressing on his brain, you cease to attach any importance to it. *But if naturalism were true then all thoughts whatever would be wholly the result of irrational causes. Therefore, all thoughts would be equally worthless. Therefore, naturalism is worthless. If it is true, then we can know no truths. It cuts its own throat.*[8]

Sometime in the '40s, Lewis said farewell to the grand theory of emergent evolution in his essay "Funeral of a Great Myth."

The Myth cannot even get going without accepting a good deal from the real sciences. And the real sciences cannot be accepted for a moment unless rational inferences are valid: for every science claims to be a series of inferences from observed facts. It is only by such inferences that you can reach your nebulae and protoplasm and dinosaurs and sub-men and cave-men at all. Unless you start by believing that reality in the remotest space and the remotest time rigidly obeys the laws of logic, you can have no ground for believing in any astronomy, any biology, any palaeontology, any archaeology. To reach the positions held by the real scientists—which are then taken over by the Myth—you must—in fact, treat reason as an absolute. *But at the same time the Myth asks me to be-*

---

[8]. "Religion Without Dogma?" in *God in the Dock*, 137, emphasis added.

lieve that reason is simply the unforeseen and unintended by-product of a mindless process at one stage of its endless and aimless becoming. The content of the Myth thus knocks from under me the only ground on which I could possibly believe the Myth to be true. *If my own mind is a product of the irrational—if what seem my clearest reasonings are only the way in which a creature conditioned as I am is bound to feel—how shall I trust my mind when it tells me about Evolution?* They say in effect "I will prove that what you call a proof is only the result of mental habits which result from heredity which results from bio-chemistry which results from physics." But this is the same as saying: "I will prove that proofs are irrational": more succinctly, "I will prove that there are no proofs": *The fact that some people of scientific education cannot by any effort be taught to see the difficulty, confirms one's suspicion that we here touch a radical disease in their whole style of thought.*[9]

In his famous essay, "Meditation in a Toolshed" (1945), he makes the point yet again: "In other words, you can step outside one experience only by stepping inside another. Therefore, if all inside experiences are misleading, we are always misled . . . . *You cannot have a proof that no proofs matter.*"[10]

9. "The Funeral of a Great Myth," in *Christian Reflections*, 88-89; emphasis added.
10. "Meditation in a Toolshed," in *God in the Dock*, 215, emphasis added.

In 1944, Lewis penned "Bulverism," his key to understanding the rotten foundations of twentieth century thought.

> The forces discrediting reason, themselves depend on reasoning. You must reason even to Bulverize. You are trying to *prove* that all *proofs* are invalid. If you fail, you fail. If you succeed, then you fail even more—for *the proof that all proofs are invalid must be invalid itself* . . . .
>
> If our inferences do not give a genuine insight into reality, then we can know nothing. *A theory cannot be accepted if it does not allow our thinking to be a genuine insight,* nor if the fact of our knowledge is not explicable in terms of that theory . . . .
>
> *A belief which can be accounted for entirely in terms of causes is worthless* . . . .
>
> All attempts to treat thought as a natural event involve the fallacy of excluding the thought of the man making the attempt.[11]

In another place, Lewis remarked on how this line of thought affected him before his conversion (1945).

> Long before I believed Theology to be true I had already decided that the popular scientific picture

---

11. "Bulverism," in *God in the Dock*, 274-275, all italics added, except for prove and proofs.

at any rate was false. One absolutely central inconsistency ruins it; it is the one we touched on a fortnight ago. The whole picture professes to depend on inferences from observed facts. Unless inference is valid, the whole picture disappears. Unless we can be sure that reality in the remotest nebula or the remotest part obeys the thought-laws of the human scientist here and now in his laboratory—in other words, unless Reason is an absolute—all is in ruins. Yet those who ask me to believe this world picture also ask me to believe that Reason is simply the unforeseen and unintended by-product of mindless matter at one stage of its endless and aimless becoming. Here is flat contradiction. They ask me at the same moment to accept a conclusion and to discredit the only testimony on which that conclusion can be based. The difficulty is a fatal one; and the fact that when you put it to many scientists, far from having an answer, they seem not even to understand what the difficulty is, assures me that I have not found a mare's nest but detected a radical disease in their whole mode of thought from the very beginning.[12]

Not much has changed. People still can't see the difficulty, and it remains a radical disease in their entire mode of thought. They cannot be brought

---

12. "Is Theology Poetry?" in *C.S. Lewis Essay Collection*, 19.

to understand that they *think* something that would make anything like *thinking* impossible.

> If, on the other hand, I swallow the scientific cosmology as a whole, then not only can I not fit in Christianity, but I cannot even fit in science. *If minds are wholly dependent on brains, and brains on biochemistry, and biochemistry (in the long run) on the meaningless flux of atoms, I cannot understand how the thought of those minds should have any more significance than the sound of the wind in the trees.*[13]

The same issue arises again in *The Abolition of Man*.

> But you cannot go on "explaining away" for ever: you will find that *you have explained explanation itself away*. You cannot go on "seeing through" things for ever. The whole point of seeing through something is to see something through it. It is good that the window should be transparent, because the street or garden beyond it is opaque. How if you saw through the garden too? It is no use trying to "see through" first principles. If you see through everything, then everything is transparent. But a wholly transparent world is an invisible world. *To "see through" all things is the same as not to see.*[14]

---

13. "Is Theology Poetry?" in *C.S. Lewis Essay Collection*, 21, emphasis added.
14. *The Abolition of Man* (1943; New York: HarperCollins, 2014), 81, emphasis added.

In the preface to *That Hideous Strength*, Lewis says that he was making the same basic point that he was making in *The Abolition of Man*. That includes this particular point we have been emphasizing. Two of the villains, Wither and Frost, got to the point of intellectual incoherence by two different routes, but they both managed to get there.

> [Speaking of Wither] It is incredible how little this knowledge moved him. It could not, because *he had long ceased to believe in knowledge itself*. What had been in his far-off youth a merely esthetic repugnance to realities that were crude or vulgar, had deepened and darkened, year after year, into a fixed refusal of everything that was in any degree other than himself. He had passed from Hegel into Hume, thence through Pragmatism, and thence through Logical Positivism, *and out at last into the complete void*. The indicative mood now corresponded to no thought that his mind could entertain. He had willed with his whole heart *that there should be no reality and no truth*, and now even the imminence of his own ruin could not wake him. The last scene of *Dr. Faustus* where the man raves and implores on the edge of Hell is, perhaps, stage fire. The last moments before damnation are not often so dramatic. Often the man knows with perfect clarity that some still possible action of his own will could yet save

him. But he cannot make this knowledge real to himself. Some tiny habitual sensuality, some resentment too trivial to waste on a blue bottle, the indulgence of some fatal lethargy, seems to him at that moment more important than the choice between total joy and total destruction. With eyes wide open, seeing that the endless terror is just about to begin and yet (for the moment) unable to feel terrified, he watches passively, not moving a finger for his own rescue, while the last links with joy and reason are severed, and drowsily sees the trap close upon his soul. So full of sleep are they at the time when they leave the right way.[15]

Wither withered because he had refused knowledge for so long that it got to the point where he could not even know *that*.

Another villain of the piece also hated knowledge, and came to the same bitter end.

[Speaking of Frost] Frost had left the dining room a few minutes after Wither. He did not know where he was going or what he was about to do. *For many years he had theoretically believed that all which appears in the mind as motive or intention is merely a by-product of what the body is doing.*

15. *That Hideous Strength* (1945; London: John Lane The Bodley Head, 1949), 438-39; emphasis added.

But for the last year or so—since he had been initiated—he had begun to taste as fact what he had long held as theory. Increasingly, his actions had been without motive. He did this and that, he said thus and thus, and did not know why. His mind was a mere spectator. He could not understand why that spectator should exist at all. *He resented its existence, even while assuring himself that resentment also was merely a chemical phenomenon.* The nearest thing to a human passion which still existed in him was a sort of cold fury *against all who believed in the mind.* There was no tolerating such an illusion. There were not, and must not be, such things as men. But never, until this evening, had he been quite so vividly aware that the body and its movements were the only reality, that the self which seemed to watch the body leaving the dining room and setting out for the chamber of the Head, was a nonentity. How infuriating that the body should have power thus to project a phantom self! (*That Hideous Strength*, 444)

Lewis touches on the point again in 1948:

You can't, except in the lowest animal sense, be in love with a girl if you know (and keep on remembering) that all the beauties both of her person and of her character are a momentary and accidental pattern produced by the collision of atoms, *and that your own response to them is only a sort of psychic phosphoresence arising from the behavior of your genes* . . . .

For one thing, it is only through trusting our own minds that we have come to know Nature herself. *If Nature when fully known seems to teach us (that is, if the sciences teach us) that our own minds are chance arrangements of atoms, then there must have been some mistake; for if that were so, then the sciences themselves would be chance arrangements of atoms and we should have no reason for believing in them.*[16]

In his essay *"De Futilitate,"* Lewis drives yet another nail in the coffin.

> It therefore follows that *all knowledge whatever depends on the validity of inference.* If, in principle, the feeling of certainty we have when we say "Because A is B therefore C must be D" is an illusion, *if it reveals only how our cortex has to work and not how realities external to us must really be, then we can know nothing whatever.*
>
> We are compelled to admit between the thoughts of a terrestrial astronomer and the behaviour of matter several light-years away that particular relation which we call truth. But this

---

16. "On Living in the Atomic Age," in *C.S. Lewis Essay Collection*, 363, 364-65; emphasis added.

> relation has no meaning at all if we try to make it exist between the matter of the star and the astronomer's brain, considered as a lump of matter. The brain may be in all sorts of relations to the star no doubt: it is in a spatial relation, and a time relation, and a quantitative relation. *But to talk of one bit of matter as being true about another bit of matter seems to me to be nonsense.*[17]

Lewis the apologist was the same man who was Lewis the husband, married to Joy Davidman. After she died, Lewis published his reflections on his grief in a small book called *A Grief Observed*. He said this about H., the abbreviation he used for his wife. Because Joy died just three years before Lewis did, this observation is right near the end of Lewis's life.

> If H. "is not," then she never was. I mistook a cloud of atoms for a person. There aren't, and never were, any people. Death only reveals the vacuity that was always there. What we call the living are simply those who have not yet been unmasked. All equally bankrupt, but some not yet declared.
>
> But this must be nonsense; vacuity revealed to whom? Bankruptcy declared to whom? To other boxes of fireworks or clouds of atoms. *I will*

---

17. "De Futilitate," in *Christian Reflections*, 62-64; emphasis added.

never believe—more strictly I can't believe—that one set of physical events could be, or make, a mistake about other sets.[18]

The year before he died, Lewis preached a sermon called "Transposition," which can be found in *The Weight of Glory*. He hammered the point yet again.

> We are certain that, in this life at any rate, thought is intimately connected with the brain. *The theory that thought therefore is merely a movement in the brain is, in my opinion, nonsense, for if so, that theory itself would be merely a movement, an event among atoms, which may have speed and direction, but of which it would be meaningless to use the words "true" or "false."* We are driven then to some kind of correspondence.[19]

After Lewis died, some of his lecture notes on the medieval cosmology were published posthumously in *The Discarded Image*, and Lewis speaks from beyond the grave.

> And now, in some extreme forms of Behaviourism, the subject himself is discounted as merely sub-

---

18. *A Grief Observed* (1961; New York: HarperOne, 2009), 28-29; emphasis added.
19. "Transposition," in *The Weight of Glory*, (1949; New York: HarperOne, 2015), 103, emphasis added.

jective; *we only think that we think. Having eaten up everything else, he eats himself up too.* And where we "go from that" is a dark question.[20]

We will finish with Lewis's essay "The Poison of Subjectivism," an essay written in 1943. Regardless of where it fits in the timeline, it lines up with everything else he said on the subject.

Up to that point, he had assumed his own reason and through it seen all other things. Now, his own reason has become the object: it is as if we took out our eyes to look at them. *Thus studied, his own reason appears to him as an epiphenomenon which accompanies chemical or electrical events in a cortex which is itself the by-product of a blind evolutionary process. His own logic, hitherto the king whom events in all possible worlds must obey, becomes merely subjective. There is no reason for supposing that it yields truth.*[21]

THE LIGHT FROM BEHIND THE SUN

And on this matter, C.S. Lewis was absolutely right. Unless reason is an absolute, all is in ruins. Moreover, we cannot say that reason is absolute without acknowledging that such a claim has

---

20. *The Discarded Image* (1964; Cambridge: CUP, 2007), 215, emphasis added.
21. "The Poison of Subjectivism," in *C.S. Lewis Essay Collection*, 657, emphasis added.

preconditions. If reason is not absolute, we can know nothing, which would include the fact that we know nothing. But if reason is absolute, how is that possible? If reason is absolute, what is it resting on? What do we mean by it?

None of this is possible unless the Word was with God and the Word was God. This is the light from behind the sun. *He* is the light from behind the sun.

These are issues that Van Til saw with extraordinary clarity. And so it is that we may call Lewis, at least when it comes to these foundational assumptions, an inadvertent presuppositionalist. But reluctant or not, he was a very effective one.

So how does this relate to other aspects of Lewis's theology? How does it relate, if at all, to the more thorough-going approach of Van Til?

CHAPTER 5
THE TAO OF LEWIS[1]

It must always be remembered that the Christian world has a distinct surplus of C.S. Lewis "wanna bees." Things have gotten to the point where any expression of appreciation for the work of Lewis can be a potential embarrassment—not because of anything said or done by Lewis himself, but rather for fear of being taken for yet another rootless American evangelical enamored of apologetics with a British accent. Nevertheless, appreciation and criticism for Lewis are both in order in the area of apologetics.

What happens if we take the sum total of the citations from Lewis in the first part of this chapter, and discuss them in the light of the two basic apologetic "schools"—evidentialism and presuppositionalism? In much that follows, I will assume

[1] Originally published in *Greyfriars Covenant: Essays on Evangelism and Apologetics* (Moscow, ID: Greyfriars Hall Press, 2001).

that the reader is familiar with the main features of that apologetic debate, and will content myself here with a brief summary.

The evidential apologist believes that there is a neutral place where a Christian may encounter an unbeliever, agree on some common ground rules, and reason from that neutral place to a faith in the God of the Bible. The presuppositional apologist, on the other hand, argues that there is no such neutral place, and that all reasoning presupposes, of necessity, the triune God of Scripture.

It is very clear that the elements of both are present in Lewis's apology for the Christian faith, but more must be said about this. For if presuppositionalism is correct, both elements are present in *every* apologist's presentation—from Alvin Plantinga to Josh McDowell, from C.S. Lewis to Norman Geisler. Given presuppositionalism, *everyone* is implicitly a presuppositionalist. This is because presuppositionalism holds that because of the necessary relationship between the Creator and all creatures, presuppositional thinking is *inescapable*. A creature must start all his reasoning with certain "givens." In fact, this entire apologetic debate could be summarized as an attempt by presuppositionalists to convince evidentialists that they are not *really* evidentialists. This being the case, it is the purpose of this essay to show, not that Lewis was implicitly presuppositional (for everyone is that), but rather that at certain key points, he was *explicitly* so.

There are also other places where he had an *explicitly* evidential approach. So this is not a fight over the body of Moses; this is no attempt to claim Lewis as a champion of presuppositionalism; rather it is simply an attempt to recognize and applaud him at those places where he went to the heart of the issue, and to critique him at those places where he did not.

BOIL IT ALL DOWN

Lewis was a master of making modern non-Christian philosophers eat their own cooking. In this regard, and to this extent, Lewis can be considered a presuppositionalist. Or, to be more precise, his critique of non-Christian philosophies required his adversaries state *their* presuppositions, and be subsequently consistent with them. Remember the proofs that there are no proofs, which is nonsense,[2] or the atheist's argument against God being the result of a bit of bone pressing on his brain.[3]

In other words, materialism is a philosophy which cannot sustain itself—materialism cannot supply the preconditions necessary for doing materialist philosophy. Lewis is not arguing here that materialism is improbable; his refutation is absolute. Materialism is *impossible*. To use his words

---

2. *Miracles*, 1st edition (New York: Macmillan, 1947), 19-20.
3. *Miracles*, 1st edition, 22.

again: "You can argue with a man who says, 'Rice is unwholesome': but you neither can nor argue with a man who says, 'Rice is unwholesome, but I'm not saying this is true.'"[4] There is no need to refute a philosophy which refutes itself. This is a key aspect of the approach which Greg Bahnsen called "the impossibility of the contrary." So those philosophies which refute *themselves* may be considered absolutely refuted.

Now this air of certainty is consistent only with a presuppositional approach. Evidentialism, in contrast, is concerned to present the Christian faith as *probably* true, as a reasonable option for reasonable men. In contrast, the presuppositional apologist says that Christianity is inescapably true. Lewis does not go this far, but he *does* say that certain unbelieving philosophies are inescapably false. And this makes at least one friend of his apologetic more than a little nervous.

> Here, I think Lewis makes one of his rare missteps in argument.... What Lewis needs to argue, and indeed does argue indirectly, is that it is overwhelmingly *more probable* that mind will be produced by a previously existing mind than by a process such as evolution....[5]

---

4. *Miracles*, 1st edition, 24.
5. Richard Purtill, *C.S. Lewis' Case for the Christian Faith* (San Francisco: Harper & Row, 1981), 26. The italics are mine.

This is a wonderful example of the hesitancy which afflicts evidentialism. It is merely *improbable* that blind purposeless chance brought our minds into existence.[6] But evidentialism grants that there is a chance, however slight, that mindless chance could have produced all the wonders of creation. Because Lewis cuts materialism no slack whatever—he says it is not improbable, it is demonstrably *false*—he is admonished for being too certain. There is a real irony here. Evidential apologists for the Christian faith want arguments for Christianity; they do not want *proofs*. Like the Israelites outside Canaan, they don't want to launch a campaign of total conquest. And even though Lewis is not at this point giving an unanswerable argument *for* Christianity, he is giving an unanswerable argument *against* one of its competitors and this, for an evidentialist, is too close for comfort.

In *Miracles*, Lewis showed that materialism cannot consistently use or talk about reason at all. In *Mere Christianity* he demonstrates that the atheist, given his premises, cannot talk about *justice*. For all who are familiar with a presuppositional approach to apologetics, this is familiar terrain. We see here an unbeliever confronted with his inability to generate ethical objections to the existence of God. So in conflict with various forms of modern unbelief,

---

6. And when asked about whether Christ was raised from the dead, a modern evidentialist could thunder, "Probably!"

Lewis lays the ax at the *root* of the tree. In Lewis's apologetic, contrary to the modern assumption, God is not in the dock—*man* is.[7]

What Lewis is doing here is discussing first principles with modern unbelievers. In the discussion, he uncovers the fact that unbelieving arguments against God are *invalid, i.e.* their conclusions do not proceed from their premises. What Lewis then does is to ask his adversaries, quite politely, to change their conclusions so that they match their premises. He is quite consistent in pointing out this surreptitious inconsistency—for yet another example, consider this blunt assessment: "The sciences bring to the 'facts' the philosophy they claim to derive from them" (*The Pilgrim's Regress*, 59, page header).

In short, Lewis was a master at the demolition of modern, unbelieving attacks on Christianity. But this presuppositional method can be taken much farther than Lewis does. For a thorough-going and consistent presuppositionalism, we must turn to Cornelius Van Til.

VAN TIL AND LEWIS

In critiquing the materialist worldview, Lewis does a fine job pointing out that the preconditions of reason are absent from the materialist view. Lewis does the fine destructive work of pointing out that

---

7. "God in the Dock," in *God in the Dock*, 244.

materialists cannot derive reason from materialism, and hence have no right to employ reason in the advancement of their case. He does not go as far as Van Til, however, in that he does not go on to state explicitly where they *do* get reason.

If materialists cannot get reason from materialism, where is it derived? The answer given by Van Til is the God of Christianity. Lewis made the case that such non-Christian philosophies could not sustain life on their own; Van Til went on to make the case that they are parasites, and that the Christian faith is the host.

Another way of stating this is to say that for Lewis the self-contradiction of materialists was an argument *against* materialism. Van Til showed how these self-contradictions by unbelievers were an inescapable argument *for* Christianity. While Lewis would say that self-contradictory philosophies need not be heeded, Van Til would say that self-contradiction is the apportioned lot of every rebellious creature, and Christ must therefore be heeded.

We may therefore set the boundaries of Lewis's limited presuppositionalism. When critiquing *modern* forms of unbelief, Lewis was negatively presuppositional. That is, he showed that the unbeliever's presuppositions could not sustain the structure which unbelief wanted to build on it. So we may consider Lewis as a *limited* presuppositional critic of modernity.

In other areas, he was not presuppositional at all. He was not presuppositional in his approach to the ancients. For example, he would not go after Plato in the same way he could critique a modern atheist. Nor was he presuppositional in his approach to modern non-Christians who were prepared to be "reasonable" as they listened to the Christian message.

THE TAO OF LEWIS

While Lewis required the unbeliever to stand on his own avowed presuppositions when attacking Christianity, he did not require this of the unbeliever when he was hearing the message of Christ presented. It is here that Lewis's compromise with the natural man is apparent. As Van Til put it,

> One can only rejoice in the fact the Lewis is heard the world around, but one can only grieve over the fact that he so largely follows the method of Thomas Aquinas in calling men back to the gospel. The "gospel according to St. Lewis" is too much of a compromise with the ideas of the natural man to constitute a clear challenge in our day.[8]

Now why would Van Til say something like this? In short, although Lewis believed fiercely in

---

8. Cornelius Van Til, *The Defense of the Faith* (Phillipsburg, NJ: Presbyterian and Reformed, 1955), 60.

objective standards of beauty, ethics, *etc.*, he also held that such standards could be, and had been, discovered everywhere, by Christian and non-Christian alike.

> If a man will go into a library and spend a few days with the *Encyclopedia of Religion and Ethics* he will soon discover the massive unanimity of the practical reason of man . . . he will no longer doubt that there is such a thing as the Law of Nature.[9]

We must be careful here. There is a great divide between proponents of an autonomous "natural law" and the proponents of "common grace." By autonomous natural law, I am referring to those who believe that natural law would be authoritative whether or not there is a God. But the cleavage is not necessarily simple to understand; suffice it to say that Lewis appeared to be saying that pagan man had a good deal of ethical common sense about him, and that if he carefully listened to Confucius or the Stoics, and ignored the modern claptrap about ethics, he could learn a great deal about true morality.

This approach caused Lewis to postulate the existence of what he called the *Tao*—the collective

---

9. "The Poison of Subjectivism," in *Christian Reflections*, 77.

moral wisdom of man.[10] His most detailed treatment of this is found in *The Abolition of Man*, which Van Til cites in this following passage.

> Lewis seeks for objective standards in ethics, in literature, and in life everywhere. But he holds that objectivity may be found in many places. He speaks of a general objectivity that is common between Christians and non-Christians and argues as though it is mostly or almost exclusively in modern times that men have forsaken it . . . . But surely this general objectivity is common to Christians and non-Christians in a formal sense only. To say that there is or must be an objective standard is not the same as to say what the standard is. And it is the *what* that is all important.[11]

Lewis appears to hold that non-Christians can have these perceptions about "natural law" on their own. Of course the Lawgiver is God, but man has the ability to discover the law that God has placed in the world—in much the same way that men can discover mathematical theorems, or a new celestial body.

But a denial of autonomous natural law does not necessitate a denial that men have a common

---

10. As a Christian, of course Lewis denied the ability of the unregenerate man to live up to this standard. But he affirmed his ability to understand it. *Christian Reflections*, 79.

11. Van Til, *Defense of the Faith*, 59.

knowledge of ethical standards. Rather, it is the conviction that men know what they know about God because of His revelation of Himself.

Now of course if men can come to search out the truth about the world (ethical or otherwise), and they can do so on their own, then there is no problem with an evidential apologetic, which simply encourages them to do so. But if God *reveals* Himself to all men—at the most fundamental level possible—then knowledge of God is a matter of God's revelation to man, and not a matter of man's discovery of God. Because Lewis strongly accepted "natural law," a necessary implication of this is that at some level he approved of an evidentialist approach or apologetic.

Lewis's approval of an evidentialist approach can be seen also in a letter he wrote, shortly before his death, to John Warrick Montgomery concerning two lectures Montgomery had delivered at the University of British Columbia. Lewis had this comment on the lectures: "Your two lectures did me good and I shall constantly find them useful. Congratulations . . . Otherwise I don't think it could be bettered."[12]

This comment of approval was made about lectures which were thoroughly in the evidentialist

---

12. John Warrwick Montgomery, *Where is History Going?* (Minneapolis: Bethany Fellowship, 1969), 222. The otherwise above refers to a minor criticism that Lewis made about Montgomery's use of the Greek word *kurios*, meaning Lord.

stream of things. Consider this statement by Montgomery from his second lecture.

> Now if you are not inclined in the direction of Christianity—as I was not when I entered university—the most irritating aspect of the line of argumentation that I have taken is probably this: it depends in no sense upon theology. It rests solely and squarely upon historical method, the kind of method all of us, whether Christians, rationalists, agnostics, or Tibetan monks, have to use in analyzing historical data.[13]

Montgomery of course is a leading proponent of the evidentialist school of apologetics; it is not surprising at all that *he* would make such a statement. What is pertinent here is Lewis's approval of this form of argument—an approval which is not at all out of step with Lewis's own approach elsewhere.[14] What Montgomery is affirming here is that his argument for Christianity depends "in no sense upon theology." Whatever else this proposition is, it

---

13. Montgomery, *Where is History Going?*, 53-54. But of course one wonders if a Tibetan monk and a Christian scholar share common ground in historical studies. Is history linear or cyclic? Why? Who says?

14. For example, see C.S. Lewis, "God in the Dock," in *God in the Dock*, 240-244. Lewis is there recounting how it is possible to allay the historical skepticism of uneducated non-Christians by simply telling them that a science called textual criticism exists, and gives us a "reasonable assurance" that some ancient texts were accurate.

is certainly a great specimen of evidentialism, and Lewis did not have a problem with it.

Now of course his acceptance of evidentialism at this point is inconsistent with his own forms of argument elsewhere. One can only speculate what would have happened if Lewis had observed a pointed collision between the evidentialism of a Montgomery and the presuppositionalism of a Van Til. For of course to say that certain areas of life can be lived without regard to theology (in this case, historical studies), is itself a theological claim—an all-encompassing theological claim.

So it appears that when non-Christians were willing to behave themselves in this "neutral zone," Lewis was quite willing to deal with them under those conditions—and talk about history, or textual criticism, or literary criticism in a reasonable, "neutral" fashion. But if the non-Christians broke the truce, and attempted to *attack* Christianity, then Lewis was prepared to deal with them at the level of their presuppositions.

C.S. Lewis was a great man, and a great scholar, but it seems that at least in this regards he was a victim of something he described well in *The Screwtape Letters*: "Your man has been accustomed, ever since he was a boy, to having a dozen incompatible philosophies dancing about together in his head."[15] In Lewis's case,

---

15. *The Screwtape Letters* (London: The Centenary Press, 1945), 11. All citations of the book are from this edition.

there were not a dozen incompatible philosophies, but only two. And they were not different philosophies of life, but rather differing philosophies of how to defend the Christian faith. Nevertheless, the contrast of differing approaches is present in Lewis's apologetic, and the contrast is stark.

REFORMED?

The presuppositional apologetic is one that flourishes in only one kind of soil—the theology of the Reformation. It can *exist* elsewhere, but it certainly cannot thrive. This may perhaps explain, at least in part, the inconsistencies in Lewis's apologetic. As a conservative Anglican, Lewis exhibits some of the theological inconsistencies of that communion. He truly was a faithful son of his church, and had his very own Elizabethan settlement going on inside his head.

> Of course reality must be self-consistent; but till (if ever) we can see the inconsistency it is better to hold two inconsistent views than to ignore one side of the evidence. The real inter-relation between God's omnipotence and Man's freedom is something we can't find out . . . We have to leave it at that. I find the best plan is to take the Calvinist view of my own virtues and other people's vices; and the other view of my own vices and other people's virtues . . . . It is plain from

Scripture that, in whatever sense the Pauline doctrine is true, it is not true in any sense which excludes its (apparent) opposite.[16]

In other words, Lewis recognizes (unlike many contemporary Christians) that Paul taught *something* about predestination, and Lewis was also prepared to say that whatever that teaching was, it was true. At the same time, he was not quite ready to spell out the content of the doctrine—he simply acknowledged its presence, and sought to guard against an unbalanced acceptance of it.

Lewis was also a classical theist—his views of God and His attributes were thoroughly orthodox. According to Lewis (and Scripture), God is not bound by time, and we cannot comprehend fully His relationship to whatever occurs within time. He would have had nothing to do with recent evangelical attempts to stake out a position halfway between classical theism and process theism.[17] But because these recent compromises are internally more consistent (just as Socinianism, a rationalistic form of non-Trinitarianism, is more consistent than Arminianism), this places Lewis in the awkward position of maintaining a "Reformed" view of God,

---

16. C.S. Lewis, *The Quotable Lewis* (Wheaton, IL: Tyndale House Publishers, 1989), 494.
17. Clark Pinnock, "Between Classical and Process Theism," in *Process Theology*, ed. Ronald Nash (Grand Rapids: Baker, 1987), 313-327.

while not pursuing some of the ramifications of that commitment. But one of the direct ramifications of this is in the field of apologetics; the result in Lewis's apologetic was inconsistency.

The reason that presuppositionalism depends upon a reformational approach should be obvious. The evidential assumption that some areas are neutral can only be sustained by a theological premise which asserts that there are some areas which God "leaves alone."[18] But if God is sovereign over all things, then there is no area which He leaves alone; there is no neutrality. And if there is no neutrality, then it is impossible to share common ground with the unbeliever as the gospel is presented.

Consequently, it is possible to speculate that perhaps Lewis was presuppositional when he was building on his orthodox belief that God is all in all—a godless universe is inconceivable (and unbelievers consequently cannot consistently build a godless universe). He did not apply this profound understanding consistently in all areas; consequently, he was quite willing to appeal to the unbeliever's reasonableness so long as the unbeliever was *not drawing attention* to his rebellion against God.

Van Til, on the other hand, was more than willing to assert that *all men* are in rebellion against

---

18. The inconsistency of Reformed evidentialists—like Warfield, Sproul, Gerstner, et al.—is not contrary to this reformational tendency. It is simply an instance of the tendency not being applied, or followed out.

God because the Bible says they are. This is assumed to be the case even when the rebellion is not apparent to us. Lewis dealt with the rebellion in a presuppositional way only *after* the rebellion was visible and apparent. Before that time, he was willing to speak to the unbeliever as one reasonable man to another.

CONCLUSION

Perhaps an allegory may be fashioned from a situation in one of Lewis's Narnia stories—*Prince Caspian*. Peter, a king of the Narnians, is in a duel with Miraz, a usurper and tyrant. In the course of the fight, Miraz falls over and Peter, a true gentleman, steps back to let him rise.

In a similar way, Lewis watches his opponents fall to the ground, and in a typical English fashion, points out that they have done so. But he is a gentleman, and he is not in a battle to the death with *all* forms of unbelief—only the aggressive ones.

In contrast to this, the consistent presuppositionalist is not in a gentlemanly duel, with agreed upon common rules. He is in a total war; he is not interested in a negotiated settlement. Like Samuel, he "hews Agag to pieces before the Lord."

CHAPTER 6

UNDRAGONED— C.S. LEWIS ON THE GIFT OF SALVATION[1]

It would be easy to represent what I am about to attempt here as part of an unseemly struggle over the body of Moses. Everybody wants a piece of Lewis—right?—and so here come the Reformed, late to the game, hindered in this particular footrace by the ball and chain of predestination. I would get rid of it, but I can't help it.

Now I don't want to be a participant in *any* unseemly struggles, retroactively claiming somebody for "our side," that somebody being now deceased.

---

1. This talk was first presented at the 2013 Desiring God Conference. It reappears here, with thanks to John Piper, Desiring God, and Crossway. Nancy and I have been to a lot of conferences, and the people at Desiring God are among the most hospitable.

I don't want to do that with anybody, much less over the venerable Lewis. I am reminded of what Lewis himself said in another context about the assured results of modern scholarship concerning the past—which, as Lewis said, were only assured results because the men involved were dead and couldn't blow the gaff.

So let me begin by noting what I am *not* seeking to do. I am not trying to represent Lewis as a doctrinaire five-pointer, or as someone in the grip of any precise system whatever. He was a churchman—not a party man, not a faction member. This disclaimer even includes the true system of doctrine that, as we all know, the archangel Gabriel delivered in 1619 to the Synod of Dort.

At the same time—and you should have known a qualification was coming—I do want to maintain that Lewis had a firm grasp of the true *graciousness* of saving grace, and that he knew that a recovery of this understanding was an essential part of the rise of classical Protestantism. When I am done, I hope that you will see Lewis as at *least* a sympathetic observer of historic Reformation theology, or—at most—an asystematic adherent of it. This latter position is the position I hold. So was C.S. Lewis small *r* reformed? Not exactly, and yes, of course.

Keep in mind that Lewis's thought developed over time. I am drawing largely from his *English Literature in the Sixteenth Century*, which was his *magnum opus*, a product of his mature thought. And while Tolkien and Lewis were lifelong friends, their friendship was strained in the latter years. Tolkien was a devout Roman Catholic, and he saw this book as an example of Lewis returning to his Belfast roots. Belfast, of course, is the largest city in *Protestant* Northern Ireland, and it was where Lewis grew up.

One other quick point should be made at the outset—concerning my qualifications even to talk about this. Am *I* Reformed? Am *I* a Calvinist? This is a point upon which I understand there has been some discussion. Well, in brief, I wish there were seven points so I could hold to the Calvinistic extras. You may count me a devotee of crawl-over-broken glass Calvinism, jet-fuel Calvinism, black-coffee Calvinism. Or, as my friend Peter Hitchens once had it, weapons-grade Calvinism. No yellow-cake uranium semi-Pelagianism for me. I buy my Calvinism in fifty gallon drums with the skull and crossbones stenciled on the side, with little dribbles of white paint running down from the corners. I get my Calvinism delivered on those fork-lift plats at Costco. I trust this reassures everyone, and I am glad we had this little chat.

ASYSTEMATIC? OR JUST MUDDLED?

It doesn't happen very often, but when it does, C.S. Lewis is perhaps the most insightful muddler you will ever read. He, along with Chesterton, has the capacity to edify you profoundly at the very moment he is saying things to make you wrench at your head in exasperation. I am thinking here of a book like *Reflections on the Psalms*. But when he is on, which is almost always, you can be done with the wrenching, and just enjoy the edification. So there's that.

Having said this, in *The Screwtape Letters*, Lewis took a jab at modern man who is accustomed to carrying around a mass of contradictions. "Your man has been accustomed, ever since he was a boy, to having a dozen incompatible philosophies dancing about together in his head" (*The Screwtape Letters*, 11). And Owen Barfield once said that Lewis himself was utterly *unlike* this, saying that what Lewis thought about everything was contained in what he said about anything.

I add this because I believe that there are many times when we are wrenching at our heads in exasperation over Lewis while the heavenly host is looking down on *us*, wrenching at their heads . . . if angels do that. There will be times when we are tempted to write off something in Lewis as a simple contradiction, when *we* are the ones who have not thought very deeply about what we are saying. Michael Ward has shown in *Planet Narnia* that Lewis could look like he was just dashing something off when he was actually building an impressive structure on deep foundations. So let us feel free to differ with him, but let's also take care not to be patronizing.

Make no mistake—Lewis had an intentional project, and that project is still a gathering river, one which shows no sign of diminishing. It is already astonishingly wide, and it is only down as far as Vicksburg. We ought not to be patronizing in how we "forgive" Lewis's little side ventures, and do some more serious thinking about how he managed to pull something like this massive project off.

HIS OWN EXPERIENCE

With all of this said in what might *appear* to be a somewhat desultory beginning, I think we should all exhort me to pull it together and try to bring in some razor sharp focus. So let's begin our discussion of Lewis's view of salvation by looking at Lewis's view of his *own* salvation.

The whole issue really boils down to how you understand the grace of God. Is salvation a cooperative affair, or does God simply intervene to bless us by taking the initiative? Was Lazarus raised from the dead in a semi-Pelagian fashion, with Lazarus pushing and Jesus pulling? Or not?

Listen to C.S. Lewis himself describing a particular moment in his own conversion.

> In a sense I was not moved by anything. I chose to open, to unbuckle, to loosen the rein. I say "I chose," *yet it did not really seem possible to do the opposite*. On the other hand, I was aware of no motives.

You could argue that I was not a free agent, but I am more inclined to think that this came nearer to being a perfectly free act than most that I have ever done. *Necessity may not be the opposite of freedom, and perhaps a man is most free when, instead of producing motives, he could only say, "I am what I do."* (*Surprised by Joy*, 224-25, emphasis mine)

Just as Ransom discovered on Perelandra, freedom and necessity are actually the same thing. In his *Letters*, Lewis had this to say about freedom and grace:

When we carry it up to relations between God and Man, has the distinction perhaps become nonsensical? After all, when we are most free, it is only with a freedom God has given us: and when our will is most influenced by Grace, it is still our will.[2]

Moving to the experience of conversion as it was experienced by others, this is how Lewis describes the experience of conversion as it was felt by "an early Protestant."[3] He says this: "All the initiative has been on God's side; all has been free, unbounded grace. And all will continue to be free, unbounded

---

2. *The Collected Letters of C.S. Lewis*, Vol. 3, 237-238 [letter to Mary Van Deusen].

3. *Oxford History of English Literature in the Sixteenth Century Excluding Drama* (1954; Oxford: OUP, 1973), 32.

grace" (*Oxford History*, 33). He is clearly in sympathy with this, for this is how *he* experienced it.

CAN'T TELL THE PLAYERS WITHOUT A SCORECARD

Now if we want to pursue this discussion, keep in mind that terms do not always stay put in history. When we refer to Calvinism today, we are usually talking about soteriology—the five points. Thus it is that a man can be a Calvinist, and also be a dispensationalist, a charismatic, or even a Presbyterian. That last one has been known to happen. I've met some.

But during the reigns of Elizabeth I and James I, identifying as a Calvinist was more about *ecclesiology*, including your view of the sacraments. In this sense, a bunch of the non-Calvinists (their sense) were all Calvinists (our sense). One of the historiographical fiascoes caused by the Oxford Movement happened as the result of their vain attempt to pretend that the Church of England was not part of the Continental Reformed community of churches—but it *manifestly* was.

Lewis was a conservative Anglican churchman, who understood the 39 Articles in their original context, and *they* were robustly Calvinistic. He was thoroughly sympathetic with theologians like Hooker, Jewel, or Andrews—who were not exactly Victorian Anglo-Catholics. They were *Protestants*, and Calvinists in a broad sense. They were a key part of the Reformed churches of Europe, which is exactly where they wanted to be. Lewis, as a literary historian, knew what they were teaching, and he identified with them. But as a natural-born irenicist, he also wanted to keep the peace for the sake of *contemporary* inter-Anglican affairs. This meant the *precise* historical nature of the founding of the Church of England sometimes got a bit blurred. But even with that said, Lewis is far more helpful on this period than many who ought to know better.

Speaking of ecclesiology, remember the vivid picture of the Church "spread out through all time and space and rooted in eternity, terrible as an army with banners" (*Screwtape Letters*, 15). And also remember that Lewis's most famous phrase—mere Christianity—is taken from Baxter, a Puritan. This is plainly Protestant ecclesiology. Some staunch Protestants may be distressed by that fact that, at the beginning of *Mere Christianity*, Lewis grants the Roman Catholics a "room" in the great house of our faith, wondering why the Catholics get a room. But we shouldn't forget that this conception of the house is a *Protestant* conception.

SOME CITATIONS

Now there are places where Lewis is critical of the Calvinists and the Puritan party in England,[4] but

---

4. E.g. *Oxford History of English Literature*, 49.

there are other places where he praises them earnestly. He refers to "the whole tragic farce which we call the history of the Reformation" (*Oxford History*, 37). Here is his snapshot description of some of the historical theology of that day:

> In fact, however, these questions [about faith and works] were raised at a moment when they immediately became embittered and entangled with a whole complex of matters theologically irrelevant, and therefore attracted the fatal attention of both government and the mob.... It was as if men were set to conduct a metaphysical argument at a fair, in competition or (worse still) forced collaboration with the cheapjacks and the round-abouts, under the eyes of an armed and vigilant police force who frequently changed sides. (*Oxford History*, 37)

With his general sympathies established, let me turn to a sample citation that seems to contradict the notion that Lewis could in any way be considered Reformed. Speaking of total depravity, he says, "I disbelieve that doctrine, partly on the logical ground that if our depravity were total we should not know ourselves to be depraved, and partly because experience shows us much goodness in human nature."[5] But of course, in this he is actually

---

5. *The Problem of Pain* (1940; New York: HarperOne, 2001), 61.

rejecting a doctrine of *absolute* depravity, which not one of us holds. But if total depravity means total inability, which it does, it would be the work of ten minutes to show that Lewis does in fact hold to it—as we shall see in a moment.

So in these sorts of formal rejections, Lewis follows his teacher Chesterton. And even Chesterton, who takes shots at Calvinism every third chance he gets, cannot stay out of the truth. For example, in *Orthodoxy* he says, "Thus he has always believed there is such a thing as fate, but such a thing as free will also."[6] Well, hey, and amen.

But the key to this is a series of statements where Lewis acknowledges that the classical Protestant position was actually in some fashion a reiteration of the Pauline teaching. Listen for that key word *Pauline*. Lewis uses it repeatedly in this context.

Under certain calm conditions, "formulae might possibly have been found which did justice to the Protestant—*I had almost said Pauline*—assertions without compromising other elements of the Christian faith" (*Oxford History*, 37).

In a letter to a Mrs. Emily McLay, he uses an illustration from quantum physics:

> I take it as a first principle that we must not interpret any one part of Scripture so that it contradicts

---

6. *Orthodoxy*, Christian Heritage Edition (1908; Moscow, ID: Canon Press, 2020), 25.

other parts . . . . The real inter-relation between God's omnipotence and Man's freedom is something we can't find out. Looking at the Sheep & the Goats every man can be quite sure that every kind act he does will be accepted by Christ. Yet, equally, we all do feel sure that all the good in us comes from Grace. We have to leave it at that. I find the best plan is to take the Calvinist view of my own virtues and other people's vices: and the other view of my own vices and other people's virtues. But tho' there is much to be puzzled about, there is nothing to be *worried* about. It is plain from Scripture that, *in whatever sense the Pauline doctrine is true*, it is not true in any sense which *excludes* its (apparent) opposite. You know what Luther said: "Do you doubt if you are chosen? Then say your prayers and you may conclude that you are."[7]

Notice him citing *Luther* here.

Lewis held that the Pauline (Protestant) doctrine is obviously true in *some* sense, but that we ought not to throw out other truths for the sake of our system. Again, amen.

And in this following citation, he thinks he has not tipped his hand—but I am afraid he has: "Theologically, Protestantism was either a recovery, or a development, or an exaggeration (it is not for

---

7. *The Collected Letters of C. S. Lewis, Vol. 3*, 354-355 [letter to Emily McLay, August 3, 1953], former emphasis mine.

the literary historian to say which) *of Pauline theology*" (*Oxford History*, 33, emphasis mine).

Lewis plainly does not believe in the Calvinistic caricatures . . . but neither do we. And when he speaks in his own voice, he says things that themselves are susceptible to the same sort of caricature. "You will certainly carry out God's purpose, but it makes a difference to you whether you serve like Judas or like John" (*The Problem of Pain*, 111).

UNDRAGONED

So let me take a moment to conduct a very brief tour of the Narnian tulip garden—a place of fond memories for me because this is where I first learned my foundational lessons in the meaning of grace. Now I admit that these are *Narnian* tulips, so they don't look quite the same as what we are used to—they are larger, for one, and they open to the sun more quickly than those that some of our stricter brethren have duct-taped shut. Nevertheless—we should be able to quickly recognize the gaudy splash of colors that characterize our floral theology. It is either the Calvinist tulip or the Arminian daisy—"He loves me, He loves me not . . ."

Eustace was miserable as a dragon, and discovered that he was utterly unable to heal himself, or prepare himself to be healed. When he tried to remove the dragon skin by himself, all he was able to do was get down underneath his dragon skin—to the *next* layer of dragon skin. And you know while you are reading this passage, beyond any shadow of any doubt, that as long as Eustace was doing his *own* scraping, it would be dragon skins all the way down.

When Peter, Susan, Edmund, and Lucy arrive in Narnia for the first time, they discover—among many other things—that four thrones were empty at Cair Paravel, empty and waiting for them. Not only that, there were prophecies about them. And in a later book, when Jill tries to explain to Aslan that they had called on him, he replies that if he had not called them, they would not have called him. The initiative is all his. "'You would not have called to me unless I had been calling to you,' said the Lion."[8]

When Aslan is killed on the Stone Table, it is for one person—the traitor Edmund. The great lion gave his life for one grimy little boy. Now it is true that Tirian in *The Last Battle* says that it was by Aslan's blood that all Narnia was saved, but while glorious, this is an application, an extension, an afterthought. The nature of the lion's death as told in the foundational story is seen as a very definite atonement. It really has to be—Lewis held to substitutionary atonement, and as Garry Williams has clearly shown in *From Heaven He Came and Sought Her*, the two doctrines are logically intertwined. He who says A may not have said B, but give him time.

---

8. *The Silver Chair* (1953; New York: HarperCollins, 1981), 24-25.

When Jill encounters Aslan in his high country, he is between her and the stream. The stream is living water, and she is nearly frantic for it. She is invited to drink, but the lion is in between. She asks if he could go away while she drinks, and is answered with a very low growl. She asks if he will promise not to do anything to her if she does come. "I make no promise," Aslan said. She then asks if he eats girls: "'I have swallowed up girls and boys, women and men, kings and emperors, cities and realms,' said the Lion" (*The Silver Chair*, 22).

She says she "daren't come and drink." "'Then you will die of thirst,' said the Lion." She resolves to go and look for another stream. "'There is no other stream,' said the Lion" (*The Silver Chair*, 23).

Now notice how Lewis brings this glorious tension to a close, and how much like his description of his own conversion it seems—"and her mind suddenly made itself up" (*The Silver Chair*, 23).

If this is semi-Pelagianism, then semi-Pelagianism has sure come a long way since I was stuck in it. This ain't your grandma's semi-Pelagianism.

When it comes to perseverance, many of us might think instantly of Susan. Is she not missing from that glorious reunion in *The Last Battle*? But I submit that this is a simple mistake. We shouldn't speculate about her final destiny unless we want Aslan to growl at us for impudent guesswork about someone else's story. But if you are still unconvinced, I would simply refer you back to an earlier chapter. Bless me, it's all in the *Institutes* . . . Bless me, what do they teach them in these schools?

THE BUOYANCY OF GRACE
Lewis plainly understands the *relief* that real grace provides. One of the most compelling factors in this discussion for me is the fact that Lewis plainly knows how salvation *tastes*:

> From this buoyant humility, this farewell to the self with all its good resolutions, anxiety, scruples, and motive scratchings, *all the Protestant doctrines originally sprang*. For it must be clearly understood that they were at first doctrines not of terror but of joy and hope: indeed, more than hope, fruition, for as Tyndale says, the converted man is already tasting eternal life. The doctrine of predestination, says the Seventeenth Article, is "full of sweet, pleasant and unspeakable comfort to godly persons" . . . . Relief and buoyancy are the characteristic notes. (*Oxford History*, 33-34, emphasis mine)

That's how it tastes. So how does it taste in a story?

STORY ALWAYS WINS
Writing a story involves high theology, and the good ones involve the kind of high theology we have been

dealing with here. It may not seem like that, but there are many theological assumptions that have to go into a rollicking good yarn. Great writers will have reflected on the reality of this, and great Christian writers tie those reflections in with what God has revealed to us about the story *He* is telling.

There are so many directions we can take with this—and we really ought to spend the rest of our lives taking them all. Story-telling is tied in with the Trinity, with the doctrine of creation, with the Incarnation, with death and resurrection, and with the great denouement of the eschaton—or to use Tolkien's great word, the final eucatastrophe.

How could we *not* be story-tellers? We worship God the Writer, God the Written, and God the Reader. How could we not create? We are created in God's image, and *He* creates. He created us so that we would do this. He came down into our world to show us how it is done; His name is Immanuel. God loves cliffhangers. He loves nail biters. On the mount of the Lord it will be provided. Exile and return stories are everywhere. So are death and resurrection stories. So are the-elder-shall-serve-the-younger stories. And the whole thing will come together at the last day, as promised in Romans 8:28, with trillions of plot points all resolved, and no remainder. And the great throng gathered before the throne will cry out, with a voice like many waters, saying, "*That* was the best story we ever heard."

Only God creates *ex nihilo*. He speaks and the cosmos springs from nothing. When we create, we are fashioning or reassembling. A carpenter works with wood, a musician with notes, an author with words. All of our material is part of the *a priori* givenness of creation. When Tolkien spoke of our story-telling as sub-creation, he acknowledged that we create from pre-existing materials—we are not God.

But if we are imitating Him rightly, we are still imitating an *ex nihilo* creation. We are reaching for something that is out of our reach—which can either be arrogant or humble, depending on whether or not we were told to reach for it.

A creature cannot imitate the Creator, and yet this is precisely what we are told to do (Eph. 5:1). Earlier in Ephesians, Paul was praying that the saints be able to comprehend things like the "breadth, and length, and depth, and height" (Eph. 3:18). He wanted them to know what couldn't be known (Eph. 3:19), speaking of the love of Christ. He wanted them to be filled with all the fullness of God (Eph. 3:19), which is like wanting the Pacific Ocean in your little thimble. *Think* of it.

For reasons having to do with His good pleasure, God has put eternity in our hearts. This is why we cannot find out what God has done, and this is also one of the ways that we are used by Him to make everything beautiful in its time: "He has made everything beautiful in its time. Also, he has put eternity into man's heart, yet so that he cannot find out what God has done from the beginning to the end" (Eccles. 3:11, ESV).

Hack writers do not sub-create a world, they simply rearrange furniture in a glibly assumed (and largely unexamined) pre-fab world. If necessary, they make it an "other world" fantasy by hanging two moons in the sky, or by naming their protagonist something like Shambilar. But this is just moving things around on the surface. There is no deep structure to it—the author is not exercising enough authority. He is being too timid. There is not enough deep structure because there is not enough deep imitation.

Michael Ward has cogently argued that one of the things that made Lewis's fiction so compelling was the element of "donegality" in it, the ability to make a place really *feel* like that place. The name came from an observation Lewis had made about the "feel" of County Donegal in Ireland. It is the reason why Narnia *tastes* the way it does. And yet Lewis accomplished this by imitating the discarded image, the medieval model of the entire solar system. He went big. When we visit Narnia, we are coming to a place that is an *artifact*. It is obviously created, and this is how the medieval observer thought about our world—for him it was not the result of a "big bang." By showing us Narnia, Lewis was reintroducing us to our own world.

If you try to create a place by simply attaching a label to it, a label that says something like "Narnia," the result will be listless, flat. If you establish the donegality through deep imitation, that atmosphere can even swallow up things that don't rightly belong there—like Mrs. Beaver's sewing machine, for instance. The problem is not the use of tools, but the use of tools that presuppose industrialization. But because of the donegality, this is scarcely noticed.

That imitation will be of the triune God, of the flow of redemptive historical theology, of Israel cascading out of Egypt, of the Lord battering down the gates of Hades. You must know—going into it—that nothing you imitate can fit in your word count. But it *will* be a world your word count can fit into.

Several other points need to be made about this. The first is that story-telling represents a *functional* Calvinism. I have emphasized the word *functional* here, because clearly there are authors, many good ones, who are not Calvinists and who might be disposed to argue this point with me. Fine, but let me make it first.

Every author stands in a *comparable* relation to the world he has created as God stands with the world *He* has created. It is comparable because, as you recall, we are imitating God. A potter is imitating God when he shapes the clay. A playwright is imitating God when he inscribes life into his characters. This is why this human relation can serve as an illustration of the divine relation. Take this illustration from Lewis, for example: "God can no more be in competition with a creature than Shakespeare can be in competition with Viola" (*The Problem of Pain*, 42).

When we are talking about a character's motivations, there are two ways we can address the question. One is internal to the structure of the play, and the other has to do with the will of the author. It makes no sense to assign 70 percent of the play to the writer, and 30 percent to the characters. The apportionment has to be 100 percent and 100 percent. And the more Shakespeare writes, the freer Viola gets. And that is what God does for us. Even Screwtape sees it—God wants beings "united to Him but still distinct" (*Screwtape Letters*, 46).

Our natural and carnal reaction is to kick against this, arguing that *they* are fictional characters without eternal souls, whereas *we* have hopes, dreams, and aspirations. We call this a poor analogy for we are much more important than the fictional characters in a play. First, this objection stands equally well (or not) against Jeremiah's comparison of the Potter and clay (Jer. 18:6). If this is a bad illustration, then so is that. Second, Lewis uses precisely this illustration. And third, and far more important, such objections reveal why our defensiveness really arises. Nobody ever says that "this is a *terrible* way to illustrate divine sovereignty. God is *much* greater than Shakespeare." But in fact, the distance between Shakespeare and God is light years greater than the distance between Dogberry and Douglas. There is a school of thought that maintains the distance between Dogberry and Douglas is just a couple of yards.

So we are greater than pots? Fine. God is much greater than any potter.

But this leads to the next point. An author is sovereign over his story, but a good author respects the ingredients and antecedents. A good author has affection and respect for his characters, and the better the author, the greater the respect. Run this out—the Almighty Author is not one who writes a novel with the flattest characters ever. No, it goes the other way. We do not just have a choice between the will of the author and the will of the character. We also must take into account the nature of the story.

And so this brings us to one last thing, a place where we modern Reformed can learn from Lewis.

CALVINISM UNDER JOVE

Reformation Calvinism was born under Jove. It flourishes under Jove, and is spiritually healthy there. We get our word *jovial* from the older view that being born under the influence of Jove would bless one with those advantages. But for the last several centuries (at least) it has come under the baneful influence of Saturn. We get our word *saturnine* in much the same way. Am I revealing here that Lewis has gotten way too much of his discarded image into my head? Will I be having dryads leading our small group Bible studies next?

Now for those who dismiss my "pagan tomfoolery"—planetary influences and theology *indeed*—with a sneer and say that *they* want a Calvinism under *Christ*, thank you, Calvinism without centaurs, the better to enable us to get back to our gospel-preserving debates about supralapsarianism, not to mention how many eggs your wife is allowed to cook on the Lord's Day, several things have to be said.

First, I would suggest (mildly) you haven't understood the point. Nobody around here has any sympathy for pagan unbelief and superstition. Christ is Lord, and only Christ. But when the point is misunderstood this way, folks haven't understood it because they are under the baneful influences of Saturn. Jove and Saturn are metaphors, but they are not *just* metaphors. The fact that you can wring out the Westminster Confession of Faith like it was a damp washcloth does not mean that you don't have a case of the saturnine jimjams. Speaking of metaphor, I fear I might be overdoing it. But I am almost done.

Second, this is not a minor issue. Just as Lucy and Susan wouldn't feel safe around Bacchus unless Aslan was around, neither do I. But I also don't feel safe around Calvinists under Saturn. Calvinism without Jesus is deadly. When these precious doctrines of ours are used to perpetuate gloom, severity, introspection, accusations, morbidity, slander, gnat-strangling, and more, the soul is not safe.

Third, the original Protestants, and the Puritans *especially*, were not at all under Saturn. Here is Lewis describing the Puritans, and it is worthwhile reflecting on why there are so many surprises in these few sentences.

> But there is no understanding the period of the Reformation in England until we have grasped the fact that the quarrel between the Puritans and the Papists was not primarily a quarrel between rigorism and indulgence, and that, in so far as it was, the rigorism was on the Roman side. On many questions, and specially in their view of the marriage bed, the Puritans were the indulgent party; if we may without disrespect so use the name of a great Roman Catholic, a great writer, and a great man, they were much more Chestertonian than their adversaries.[9]

Where did *that* come from? It came from Lewis's thorough acquaintance with the primary sources left to us by *our* fathers, and that legacy is a large

---

9. *Selected Literary Essays*, ed. Walter Hooper (Cambridge: CUP, 1969), 116.

contributor to my willingness to luxuriate in my quite oxymoronic goal of becoming and remaining a Chestertonian Calvinist.

And fourth, with this as the good news, over the last generation, there have been a number of indications that our self-imposed saturnine exile may be coming to an end. Many Calvinists are again becoming jovial—which should not be reduced to a willingness to tell the occasional joke. The issue is much deeper than that—we are talking about rich worship, robust psalm-singing laden with harmonies, laughter and Sabbath-feasting, exuberant preaching, and all with gladness and simplicity of heart. The winter is breaking. This is not just a thaw, but promises to be a real spring.

CHAPTER 7
WAS C.S. LEWIS REFORMED?

The answer to the question posed by the title is, of course, *not exactly*. At the same time, and in a different sense, the answer is *yes, of course*. And this means that while there is substantive agreement, there is a clear difference between how some of the modern Reformed articulate the truth on certain issues and how Lewis did. And I want to suggest, in saying this, that many modern Reformed pastors, in some key areas, have something to learn about all this from Lewis.

First, C.S. Lewis did believe in predestination, and he did so without weaseling off the central point. He refused to set one truth against another. He asserted this:

> Of course reality must be self-consistent; but till (if ever) we can see the consistency it is bet-

ter to hold two inconsistent views than to ignore one side of the evidence . . . . It is plain from Scripture that, in whatever sense the Pauline doctrine is true, it is not true in any sense which *excludes* its (apparent) opposite.[1]

It is important here to note how Lewis named the doctrine of predestination, under discussion, the "Pauline doctrine." And he assumed it was true in *some* sense which would make people think it *might* exclude its apparent opposite—the genuine freedom of men and women. But of course, because God cannot lie, no truths contradict at the ultimate level. God is sovereign and the creature is free.

As his *magnum opus* on English literature made clear, C.S. Lewis understood this as the basic reason for the exuberance of the early Reformation.

> From this buoyant humility, this farewell to the self with all its good resolutions, anxiety, scruples, and motive scratchings, all the Protestant doctrines originally sprang. For it must be clearly understood that they were at first doctrines not of terror but of joy and hope: indeed, more than hope, fruition, for as Tyndale says, the converted man is already tasting eternal life. The doctrine of predestination, says the XVIIth Article, is "full

---

1. *The Collected Letters of C.S. Lewis, Vol. 3*, 355 [letter to Emily McLay, August 3, 1953], emphasis in original.

of sweet, pleasant and unspeakable comfort to godly persons." . . . Relief and buoyancy are the characteristic notes. (*Oxford History*, 33-34)

Lewis's thorough-going sympathy with this is hard to miss.

Lewis does not deny genuine human freedom (just as the Westminster Confession does not), but he steadfastly refused to place either the doctrine of sovereignty or the doctrine of genuine freedom on the Procrustean bed of the other one. This refusal looks like compromise to the hyper-Calvinists of this world, and it certainly seems inconsistent to the cold rationalism of Arminianism. But it is nevertheless the Reformed confessional position. As Ransom discovered on Perelandra, freedom and necessity are the same thing. One of Lewis's favorite theologians was the Elizabethan Anglican, Richard Hooker, who was a thorough-going Protestant on the doctrines of grace.

The 39 Articles, cited by Lewis above, are a wonderful statement of Reformation faith, and Lewis was a conservative churchman who understood the original context of those articles—which is more than can be said about many of those who subscribe to them today. He understood the efficacy of grace, the sovereignty of grace, the *graciousness* of grace. When Jill wanted to come to the water, she mentioned that she had called to Aslan. But Aslan said she would not have called him unless she had been called *by* him.

Now, what does it matter? This is not written so that we might have a fight with Anglo-Catholics and modern evangelicals over the body of Moses. This is said so that our TRs, the truly reformed among us, might be encouraged to learn something they really need to learn. C.S. Lewis has a lot to teach hard-line five pointers—but abandoning the five points is not the lesson. Someone once made a wonderful point about Lewis generally, that he made righteousness readable. In the same way, he made the doctrines of predestination and justification wash over a sinner with sweet relief. He did not do this with our wretched "seeker friendly" way of dumbing everything down in a condescending way. He did not confound intelligence with unintelligibility, and he did not confuse intelligibility with baby talk. He presupposed the intelligence of the reader, and wrote to it.

This is not to endorse every single thing C.S. Lewis may have written, particularly on this very topic. But the truths Lewis presents are readable, understandable, and altogether lovely. He loved the truths he presented, and was a man of such giftedness that he made what he loved lovely.

And in this, many pastors in the orthodox Reformed tradition need to learn this particular lesson. More beauty in wordsmithing does not lessen the amount of truth that words carry, but rather increases it drastically. The beautiful words Naphtali speaks do not displace content-bearing words. A pearl necklace on a beautiful woman is not extraneous.

A man who is called to the use of words, as ministers are, and who ignores the aesthetic aspect of them in order to concentrate on "truth" is actually at war with the truth. Instead of a pearl necklace he gives the beautiful woman a dog collar—and then pretends he did it because he loves and respects the woman.

So was Lewis reformed? The answer comes back in a way that I think he would appreciate. The answer is *kind of*.

> In *Hamlet* a branch breaks and Ophelia is drowned. Did she die because the branch broke or because Shakespeare wanted her to die at that point in the play? Either—both—whichever you please. The alternative suggested by the question is not a real alternative at all—once you have grasped that Shakespeare is making the whole play.[2]

C.S. Lewis was not just a winsome and engaging writer, a popularizer of theological topics. He was

---

2. "The Laws of Nature," in *God in the Dock*, 79.

also a prophetic writer who saw and understood the foundational issues.

In *That Hideous Strength*, Ransom says this about the inhabitants of Sulva, our moon.

> On this side, the womb is barren and the marriages are cold. There dwell an accursed people, full of pride and lust. There when a young man takes a maiden in marriage, they do not lie together, but each lies with a cunningly fashioned image of the other, made to move and to be warm by devilish arts, for real flesh will not please them, they are so dainty (*delicati*) in their dreams of lust. Their real children they fabricate by vile arts in a secret place. (*That Hideous Strength*, 337)

Seventy years ago, Lewis knew more about virtual sex, and robosex, and the rising tide of pornification that is gradually submerging our culture, than do many Christian leaders today, alive in the time when it is actually happening to us. The issue is not knowledge of the technology; the issue is knowledge of the heart of man. And what cannot be seen with a prophetic heart will never be seen with non-prophetic eyes.

Let me set a scenario twenty years from now and ask what should be done about it in the courts of the church. And then, having rendered what you think the decision ought to be, try to work through a detailed and reasoned defense of that decision.

A woman in your congregation wants to file for divorce because she discovered that her husband, while away on a business trip, visited a sexual theme park, at which place he was hooked up to a contraption that enabled him to have virtual sex to the point of climax with his choice of porn stars, or even with cartoon characters. The husband admits the visit, but says it was "just entertainment." The wife insists that it was adultery, pure and simple, and that she has biblical grounds for a divorce. Do you grant permission for the divorce? Further, if the man remains unrepentant, do you excommunicate him for his sexual uncleanness? The answer, in case you were wondering, is *yes* and *yes*. Do the answers change if his escapade was with Jessica Rabbit? The answer is *no*, it doesn't.

The case is extreme, and in order to defend our answer we will have to show our work. I should add that while the case seems extreme now, it won't seem that way twenty years out.

But we shouldn't give such easy answers because we have flattened all things sexual into one all-purpose sin. There really is a difference, for example, between lawful erotica and porn. The writer of the Song of Solomon wrote some poetry that insinuated *his* sexual imagination into the sexual experience of other people, and these other people, the readers, were not married to him. There is therefore a lawful use of sexual imagination that encompasses more than two married people with the bedroom door closed. But what is the line?

In the making of actual porn, actual people are involved, and their involvement is sin. That means the consumption of such porn for personal gratification involves the consumer in the same sin, extending it by means of his voyeurism. But a sex scene in a novel is different—I am not saying it is necessarily better, but rather that it is different. In such a case, the additional participant is the imagination of the author. The same thing goes for animated work—no actual people are represented in the final product. At the same time, an actual person, the animator, is very much involved. The same principle extends to the software engineers and technicians who build sexbots or cyber-cathouses.

A child's joke asks what the difference is between a mailbox and a hippopotamus. "I don't know, what is it?" "Well, I sure am not going to send *you* to mail any letters!"

A written sex scene, designed to entice a reader into a "follow-your-heart" ethic, even if adulterous, is wicked, even if it is not very steamy. Another sexual scene, designed to exalt marital love, and which successfully does so without luring the reader into envy and discontent, is entirely lawful. The issue is not the presence or absence of someone else's sexual imagination. The issue is whether that imagination is governed by God's standards for the world.

So arts are lawful. Imagination in the realm of sexual matters is also lawful. It becomes unlawful when they are *devilish* arts. It becomes unlawful when they are *wicked* imaginations. If you don't know the difference, then we are not going to send you to mail any letters for us.

"There are many devices in a man's heart; Nevertheless the counsel of the Lord, that shall stand" (Prov. 19:21).

"Lo, this only have I found, that God hath made man upright; but they have sought out many inventions" (Eccles. 7:29).

What is the purpose? What is the end? What is the point? Let us end this meditation with two quotations, one from Lewis and the other from the apostle Paul:

> Literature exists to teach what is useful, to honour what deserves honour, to appreciate what is delightful. The useful, honourable, and delightful things are superior to it: it exists for their sake; its own use, honour, or delightfulness is derivative from theirs. (*The Discarded Image*, 214)

> Finally, brethren, whatsoever things are true, whatsoever things are honest, whatsoever things are just, whatsoever things are pure, whatsoever

things are lovely, whatsoever things are of good report; if there be any virtue, and if there be any praise, think on these things. (Phil. 4:8)

Accept this principle, and do as you please.

C.S. Lewis was a writer who was acutely aware of the liberating power of grace. When grace has come to dominate someone, they do not come across to others as . . . dominated.

The paradox was stated well by John Donne.

Take me to you, imprison me, for I,
Except you enthrall me, never shall be free.[3]

And it was a paradox that Lewis refers to repeatedly over the course of his books, fiction and non-fiction alike. Men and women who are under grace are men and women who are liberated—because they are no longer striving to grasp their own personality, they are simply given their personality. All of grace, all gift.

Speaking of Mark Studdock in *That Hideous Strength*, Lewis makes this observation:

> He wondered vaguely why he was like that. How did other people—people like Denniston or

---

3. Holy Sonnet: Batter my heart, three-person'd God, lines 12-13. See *Poems by John Donne*, Christian Heritage Edition (1633; Moscow, ID: Canon Press, 2021), 32.

Dimble—find it so easy to saunter through the world with all their muscles relaxed and a careless eye roving the horizon, bubbling over with fancy and humor, sensitive to beauty, not continually on their guard and not needing to be? What was the secret of that fine, easy laughter which he could not by any efforts imitate? Everything about them was different. They could not even fling themselves into chairs without suggesting by the very posture of their limbs a certain lordliness, a leonine indolence. There was elbow room in their lives, as there had never been in his. (*That Hideous Strength*, 447)

To a man wound tight in self and sins, grace looked unbelievably relaxed. And in *The Horse and His Boy*, Shasta had an almost identical experience. Having grown up as a virtual slave, under a harsh and uncaring master, Shasta had no idea of what true nobility might look like.

And they were not dressed like men of Calormen. Most of them had legs bare to the knee. Their tunics were of fine, bright, hardy colors—woodland green, or gay yellow, or fresh blue. Instead of turbans they wore steel or silver caps, some of them set with jewels, and one with little wings on each side. A few were bare-headed. The swords at their sides were long and straight, not curved like Calormene scimitars. And instead of being grave and mysterious like most Calormenes, they walked with a swing and let their arms and shoulders go free, and chatted and laughed. One was whistling. You could see that they were ready to be friends with anyone who was friendly and didn't give a fig for anyone who wasn't. Shasta thought he had never seen anything so lovely in his life. (*The Horse and His Boy*, 54-55)

There is a realm *beyond* the gates of obligation, and it is the task of grace to get us there. Sin and rebellion fall short of that gate, or run the other way. But mere duty can only get us up to the gate where we clutch the iron bars, and gaze wistfully in.

It is very bad to reach the stage of thinking deeply and frequently about duty unless you are prepared to go a stage further. The Law, as St. Paul first clearly explained, only takes you to the school gates. Morality exists to be transcended. We act from duty in the hope that someday we shall do the same acts freely and delightfully.[4]

Duty can prop us up, and it might even look to others as though we were standing. But grace contrasts with this, and it does not just contrast with it on the pages of a theological dictionary. The contrast

---

4. "The Novels of Charles Williams," in *C.S. Lewis Essay Collection*, 576.

comes in how it tastes. Lewis describes this when he is summarizing the doctrines of the early Protestants.

> Bliss is not for sale, cannot be earned. "Works" have no "merit," though of course, faith, inevitably, even unconsciously, flows out into works of love at once. He is not saved because he does works of love: he does works of love because he is saved. It is faith alone that has saved him: faith bestowed by sheer gift. From this buoyant humility, this farewell to the self with all its good resolutions, anxiety, scruples, and motive-scratchings, all the Protestant doctrines originally sprang. (*Oxford History*, 34)

From the use Lewis makes of words and phrases like *anxiety*, *scruples*, and *motive-scratchings*, it is easy to tell where his sympathies lie. Lewis deeply admired those free souls who were comfortable in their own skin, and who managed to live morally while being comfortable in their own skin. Lewis admired those who used their liberty in the pursuit of a holy happiness. He did not admire wowsers.

And the early Protestants were, for him, a classic exhibit of what the power of grace could accomplish.

> Relief and buoyancy are the characteristic notes.... It follows that nearly every association which now clings to the word *puritan* has to be eliminated when we are thinking of the early Protestants.

> Whatever they were, they were not sour, gloomy, or severe; nor did their enemies bring any such charge against them . . . . Protestantism was not too grim, but too glad, to be true. (*Oxford History*, 34)

But in one of the most successful historical slanders ever accomplished, one of the best words for describing Lewis's *bete noire* in this is the word *puritanical*. That word now represents something that is almost 180 degrees out from what the original Puritans were like. If you say today that someone is puritanical, it means they are wound tight. They are a stuffed shirt, an abstinent prig, a stern taskmaster, a Gradgrind.

But . . .

> But in reality Puritanism and the Counter-Reformation, or even Puritanism and the Middle Ages, were on this point in positions almost opposite to those that moderns imagine for them. Asceticism is far more characteristic of Catholicism than of the Puritans. Celibacy and the prise of virginity are Catholic; the honour of the marriage bed is Puritan. Milton was being typically Puritan when he wrote, something too excessively, of the loves of Adam and Eve.[5]

Grace does not mean that we now get to sin. Grace means that we are liberated from the bondage to

---

5. *Studies in Medieval and Renaissance Literature* (Cambridge: CUP, 1966), 117.

sin, which is in fact the deepest bondage. Some like to maintain that we are no longer "under the law, but under grace." This is quite true, as the apostle Paul said it.

"For sin shall not have dominion over you: for ye are not under the law, but under grace" (Rom. 6:14).

But he also says that being under grace means that sin "shall not have dominion over you." Being under law meant that we were constantly under the condemnation of the law because the law would provoke our sinful natures such that we would compulsively sin, and thereby hold us in a perpetual state of condemnation. Being under law did not mean that we didn't get to sin. It meant that we couldn't stop sinning.

Being under grace brought in sweet relief, like a breeze in a high mountain meadow. And returning to Lewis's earlier illustrations, it affected everything, from how you sit in a chair to how you walk down a Calormene street.

> Long my imprisoned spirit lay
> Fast bound in sin and nature's night;
> Thine eye diffused a quickening ray,
> I woke, the dungeon flamed with light;
> My chains fell off, my heart was free,
> I rose, went forth, and followed Thee.[6]

6. Charles Wesley's "And Can It Be."

So was Lewis Reformed? No—if you want to know if he was a card-carrying member of TULIPs Anonymous. But he was well read in the literature, and on the basic issues, he was certainly informally Reformed.

CHAPTER 8
THE RANSOM TRILOGY

One of the great ironies surrounding the publication and continued popularity of Lewis's space trilogy is the fact that everybody still calls it the space trilogy. If there was one thing that C.S. Lewis wanted people to quit calling the heavens, it would be *space*. Space makes us think of vast expanses, full of nothing but dead blackness, punctuated here and there by shapeless asteroids and inchoate oceans of flaming gas.

In fact, the popular concept of "space" has actually resulted in many moderns imagining it to be something pretty close to the biblical description of damnation—the outer darkness. This should perhaps indicate to us that one of Screwtape's relatives was likely involved in all of this, with the result that things heavenly have come to have hellish connotations for us. Something has gone seriously wrong somewhere.

This was in fact one of the dragons that Lewis came to slay, and yet for some reason his publishers continue to put "space trilogy" on these books. Contrast this with the experience that Ransom had when he was first becoming acclimatized to the "heavens."

> But Ransom, as time wore on, became aware of another and more spiritual cause for his progressive lightening and exultation of heart. A nightmare, long engendered in the modern mind by the mythology that follows in the wake of science, was falling off him. He had read of "Space": at the back of his thinking for years had lurked the dismal fancy of the black, cold vacuity, the utter deadness, which was supposed to separate the worlds. He had not known how much it affected him till now—now that the very name "Space" seemed a blasphemous libel for this empyrean ocean of radiance in which they swam.[1]

Apart from the collision that results with Lewis's vision, there is also the fact that the phrase is actually not descriptive enough. How many science fiction writers have there been to date? And how many of them have produced trilogies? Many of them cannot be *kept* from producing trilogies. So the chances are pretty good that the number of space trilogies can

---

1. *Out of the Silent Planet* (1938; New York: Scribner, 2009), 34.

be reckoned by the score, and yet, such is Lewis's continued authorial dominance that his remains *the* space trilogy. If we are fortunate, we may be able to create some room for the others.

So words do matter, but they do not matter as much as the vision behind the words matters. Even though "space trilogy" is emblazoned right there on my set of the three books, the fact remains that Lewis has nevertheless opened up the heavens for countless readers. I am not speaking here of Heaven—although Lewis is responsible for large numbers of people coming to understand *that* better as well. Not only so, but he is also responsible for a large number of people *going* there. His vision of Heaven, as seen for example in *The Last Battle* and *The Great Divorce*, is a subject worth considering in its own right, but I am concerned here with Lewis and the heavens.

The final Heaven and the heavens we can see at night are not two separated subjects. They are closely related to one another. To the ancient and medieval eye what we could see in the night sky was not the ultimate Heaven, obviously not. But what we could see was thought of as the anterooms of Heaven, the outskirts. We were like sailors centuries ago approaching the coasts of an undiscovered and unexplored Chinese empire, knowing that the great rumors were still only fables to us. The capital city with its "stately pleasure dome" was still out of sight. What we had heard about was still far inland, if it existed at all. When we first made landfall, we could see none of that. But we could see the coastland. We could see *that* with our own eyes.

Has any mortal seen Heaven? Well, actually, all of us have seen the outskirts.

If you ask a typical modern if he has ever seen an angel, you will likely get laughed at. You are likely to get this treatment even if the modern you ask happens to be a professing Christian. "Seeing angels" is something our more excitable brethren on the charismatic fringes do, and *we* by contrast are sober, responsible, upright, not drunk, and pretty duddy. And so when one of these buttoned-up-tight Christians tells you that he has never seen an angel, has it ever occurred to you to point at the night sky and ask, "So what are those?"

After you have worked through the initial consternation, and the "are you serious?" follow up questions, you will have yourself a serious cosmological discussion. And Lewis was deadly serious about provoking such discussions. It was an essential part of his project.

> "In our world," said Eustace, "a star is a huge ball of flaming gas."
>
> "Even in your world, my son, that is not what a star is but only what it is made of." (*The Voyage of the Dawn Treader*, 209)

I own an older version of *The New Bible Dictionary*, and in the entry for Host of Heaven, the writer is talking about the identification of celestial beings and celestial bodies, and he says this:

> No doubt to the Heb. mind the distinction was superficial, and the celestial bodies were thought to be closely associated with heavenly beings. In fact, the implied angelology of C.S. Lewis's novels (*Out of the Silent Planet, etc.*) would probably have commended itself with some force to the biblical writers.[2]

The heavenly host refers to God's armies, and it also refers to the stars in all their vast array. What we are looking at through our telescopes is not the debris field and leftover gasses from a large and rather unfortunate explosion. "Lord Sabaoth is his name/ from age to age the same/and He must win the battle." Lord Sabaoth means Lord of hosts, Lord of the armies, Lord of all the stars.

We have trained ourselves in a deliberate form of intellectual schizophrenia. We believe in the modern cosmology, just as it was handed to us in our science classes and Star Wars movies, and if we are conservative evangelicals, we *also* believe in the account of the Star of Bethlehem, and the message

---

2. J.D. Douglas, ed., *The New Bible Dictionary* (Grand Rapids: William B. Eerdmans, 1962), 543.

delivered by the host of heaven to the shepherds keeping watch over their flocks by night. It never once occurs to us to try to put all those things together in one coherent whole. And if some aspiring liberal presses us on the Star of Bethlehem, we defend ourselves by retreated to something called "the spiritual realm," which is something like the 17th dimension. The main virtue of this place is that nothing can be falsified there: "Your man has been accustomed, ever since he was a boy, to having a dozen incompatible philosophies dancing about together inside his head" (*The Screwtape Letters*, 11).

The distance from Jerusalem to Bethlehem is about 6 miles. Herod's scholars sent the wise men to Bethlehem on the basis of Micah 5:2, but it was a *star* that led the wise men to a particular house in that same town. Now if the Bible is the Word of God, without error in all that it affirms, then stars are not what we have all been quietly assuming them to be. Either the wise men were doing some serious astrological math on the backs of camels in the dark, or a star stopped over the right house, say fifty feet up. If the former, then astrology is valid, and if the latter, then a star is not millions of miles in diameter, for that would have burned all of Bethlehem, and our entire planet, to a cinder. The solution, for those who are prepared to read Lewis sympathetically, from Narnia to *The Discarded Image*, from *The Discarded Image* to the descent of the gods on Ransom's bedroom, is straightforward, obvious, and manifestly biblical.

And that goes double for the angels who announced peace on earth, good will toward men. Angels, stars, Oyarsa, all the same kind of thing. When Luke tells us that the angels went away from them back into heaven (Luke 2:15), it would perhaps be best to visualize them as *thwapping* back into their spots, kind of like what the stars do in Star Trek whenever the ship goes into hyperdrive. Not that we put any exegetical weight on that.

CHAPTER 9
THE SHADOW OF THAT HYDDEOUS STRENGTH[1]

In his very insightful book *Experiment in Criticism*, C.S. Lewis advanced a novel approach to evaluating the quality of literature. Instead of putting the book in question under a microscope, and examining it with the eye of the trained critic, established criteria in hand, he suggested that we put the average reader of that book, or of that kind of book, across from us in a comfortable chair, and have a discussion with him about it.

This might not be an actual conversation, and be more of a thought experiment, but you still get the idea. The study of literature involves more than studying the intent of the author—it includes also studying the intent of the readers. And in this

1.This essay first appeared in *Credo*, March 11, 2020.

proposal of his, Lewis identifies two different kinds of reader, who in their turn help us identify the different kinds of writers.

This approach led Lewis to suggest a book that a reader returns to again and again is a book that should be treated as an artifact which contains something valuable. The kind of "just-kill-the-time-on-an-airplane" book, the kind you find clogging up airport bookstores, is a consumption item—like a package of Ding Dongs purchased at a convenience store. You use it for its very temporary purpose, and then throw the delivery platform away. It is the kind of book you might find at a garage sale in a cardboard box, filled with similar books, and tagged at fifty cents for the lot.

Of course, we can't be *too* strict with this airport illustration, in that Lewis himself purchased a book that was a genuine milestone in his life—MacDonald's *Phantastes*—at a train station when he was a teenager. Just think how different twentieth century Christianity would have been if he had purchased *Last of the Breed* by Louis L'Amour instead.

Now judged by this most admirable criterion, *That Hideous Strength* constitutes a formidable presence in my life. I have read it somewhere around fifteen times, and so I might want to take Lewis's standard up a notch. He argued a book was worthwhile if someone could return to it again and again, and each time find the return visit amply rewarded.

This has certainly been true in my experience, but my relationship with *That Hideous Strength* actually goes well beyond that. My situation is such that I find that if I haven't read it for a while, I *must* return to it. And I expect to feel this way about it until the river Jordan is up at least to my knees.

But *why*? One of the great novels of the twentieth century was *That Hideous Strength*. It is a fantastic read as a straightforward story, but that is not where the greatness lies. I would be hard pressed to come up with a more *prophetic* book than this one. The way things have unfolded in the six decades since he wrote has been nothing short of astonishing.

THE ABOLITION OF MAN AND THAT HIDEOUS STRENGTH

Owen Barfield once said that what Lewis thought about everything was contained within what he said about anything. This is simply a way of describing what integrated worldview thinking is like, and Lewis certainly provides us with a good example. But in the case of Lewis, there are times when the fact he operates this way is far more evident than at other times. The publication of *That Hideous Strength,* and the company it keeps, points to one of those times.

To begin with, *The Abolition of Man* and *That Hideous Strength* really need to be treated as companion volumes. In his preface to *THS*, which Lewis wrote in 1943, he says this: "This is a 'tall story' about devilry, though it has behind it a serious 'point' which I have tried to make in my *Abolition of Man*" (*That Hideous Strength*, 7).

The only thing to take issue with here is his use of the word *tried*. He didn't *try* to make this serious point; he made it—fully, seriously, compellingly. And the need for us to understand that particular point has not diminished in any way in the decades since. In these two books, Lewis does not just write from "within the Tao," but rather from within the depths of the Tao. That word *Tao* is the word Lewis uses to describe the system of ethics that the human race holds in common.

This is how he sees things in 1943 concerning our time that we have trouble seeing now. He saw the storm when it was the size of a man's fist, and we are in the midst of the typhoon, and we want to call it sunbathing weather.

And Alan Jacobs has helpfully pointed out that this particular intersection of thought involved more than just these two works.

> His key insight into this genealogy [of science and magic] may be found in the bravura introduction to the history of English poetry and prose in the sixteenth century, a book that he agreed to write in 1935 but did not complete until 1953. Along the way he condensed some of that project's major themes into the 1944 Clark

Lectures at Cambridge, and those themes overlap strongly with those of his novel *That Hideous Strength*, which he began at the end of 1942, just as he was writing the Riddell lectures [the basis for *Abolition*] . . . . It is therefore helpful to explore *The Abolition of Man* in conjunction with these other texts that are so closely related to it.[2]

Now as it happens, I have read *The Abolition of Man* almost as many times as I have read *That Hideous Strength*, and this cannot really be described as coincidental. And so it may dangerous for me to point to a few objects of interest in texts that I am claiming would actually repay a lifetime of return visits, as though what I am pointing to might exhaust the treasure to be found there. So if you will permit me to wave off any such notion, I will then feel free to point to a small handful of things that I believe relate to the essential point.

In *Abolition*, Lewis points out how science and alchemy were born at the same time, and in the same neighborhood:

> The serious magical endeavor and the serious scientific endeavor are twins: one was sickly and died, the other strong and throve. But they were twins . . . .

---

2. Alan Jacobs, *The Year of Our Lord 1943: Christian Humanism in an Age of Crisis* (Oxford: OUP, 2018), 132.

> It might be going too far to say that the modern scientific movement was tainted from its birth: but I think it would be true to say that it was born in an unhealthy neighbourhood and at an inauspicious hour. (*The Abolition of Man*, 76, 78)

In *That Hideous Strength*, we find these separated twins are reunited. The evil forces of the N.I.C.E. are supreme technocrats, using the machinery of bureaucratized science and technology to mow down anything that gets in their way, and it appears that what is getting in their way is anything distinctly *human*. Their whole enterprise is undertaken in the name of Science, all rise. But as they pursue the implications of their scientific revolution, they find that they are doing the bidding of "macrobes," their pseudo-scientific name for what are actually powers of the air, which is to say, devils. They have come full circle. By declaring war on all that was truly spiritual in man, they invited in all that was truly "spiritual" in the ranks of fallen angels. The scientist has become the magician; the mad scientist has become the necromancer.

With this as the background framework for understanding the novel, there are three basic themes in the book I would like to emphasize. The first is authority and submission in marriage, and how defiance and surrender can both be indicative of a genuine repentance. The second is Lewis's understanding of relativism as a corrosive that eats out any container you might want to keep it in. Western culture, like Mark Studdock, has been locked in the Objective Room. The third point is the centrality of Christ.

DEFIANCE AND SURRENDER

That Hideous Strength begins with the word *matrimony*, and the whole thing is as robust a defense of that holy estate as you will find anywhere. But we begin with Jane's disillusionment with marriage, after only six months of it.

The story revolves around the separate tracks of Mark and Jane Studdock, recently married, and quite unhappily so. They both contribute significantly to their shared unhappiness, and each one does so by missing the point of two other essays that Lewis wrote around this same time.

Mark Studdock would have profited greatly by reading "The Inner Ring," as that essay describes in great detail the devil that drives him. *That Hideous Strength* makes the same point that the essay does through a long and sustained narrative, with Mark being the walking embodiment of the lust described. Mark is tantalized, constantly, by the prospect and opportunity of being included in the "next" inner circle, and that ravenous lust to be included is the center of his life. "The Inner Ring" is included in *The Weight of Glory* and was originally an oration presented at King's College in 1944, the year after *THS* was published.

And as Alan Jacobs has noted, Jane would have profited by reading "Membership," also included in *The Weight of Glory*. In that address, Lewis examines what it really means to belong to one another, and what true organic relationships are actually supposed to be like. The true "belonging" that he describes there is Jane's *bête noire*, as the French would say. An American would say that the very idea of belonging like that gave her the fantods.

Mark is driven by a desire to get *in*, whatever the cost, and Jane is consumed by her desire to stay *out*, at all costs. His desire to belong to the progressive element, or to the smart set, or to the next sparkling group that is really in the know, is a desire that has already cost him the genuinely valuable friendships that he used to have, and is an important part of the reason why his marriage to Jane is so strained.

For Jane's part, she does not want to surrender herself, to give herself up. This reluctance is important to the plot of the book because her strong desire not to give herself to motherhood "just yet" is the reason why the birth of a great deliverer for Britain had been prevented. And because, as Ransom notes, submission is an "erotic necessity," her unwillingness to surrender herself completely is another contributor to the tensions in her marriage to Mark (*That Hideous Strength*, 179). And though she wants to be *with* the "nice" people at St. Anne's, she is very reluctant to join them as a member of their company. She is most reluctant to be "taken in." She wants to be with them, but would much prefer to be with them on her own terms.

So the contrast between Mark and Jane Studdock is stark. His life is consumed with a lust to be part of the "inner ring," his whole life a yearning, a striving, to be included in the group that really matters. And each time he makes it into the object of his ache, he discovers yet another circle keeping him out. Further down, and further in.

Jane's particular form of selfishness is the opposite kind. She does not want to be included, or as she might call it, *absorbed*. She wants to be sure to maintain her own identity, her own autonomy. She is arch and prim in her feminism, and by that means has guaranteed her own unhappiness.

And so because both Mark and Jane must be converted in the course of the story, this means they must repent of their respective sins—and these acts of repentance have to move in opposite directions. Mark must repent of his craven desire to be included, and this is why his repentance is marked by his act of rebellion. And Jane must repent of her desire to hang onto her own identity, and so her conversion is a striking act of submission, a surrender of that rebellion.

As part of his training in "objectivity," Mark is being required by Frost to trample on the face of a crucifix. And when he finally comes to his breaking point, he says, "It's all bloody nonsense, and

I'm damned if I do any such thing" (*That Hideous Strength*, 418). He is the end product of what Lewis identifies in *Abolition* as a truly destructive form of education. And as that end product, he is one more unit in a vast regiment of "men without chests." And so when *he* comes to the point of repentance, it takes the form of *rebellion*. "It's all bloody nonsense, and I'm damned if I do any such thing." And the angels burst into song.

As for Jane, she is walking outside the manor at St. Anne's. "Then, at one particular corner of the gooseberry patch, the change came" (*That Hideous Strength*, 394).

She had been the end product of *her* form of education. In the name of advancing the position of women, she discovers that what this approach to education actually does is degrade women into something else. A first-rate woman is transformed into a third-rate man. She is hard, brittle, touchy, and most miserable. And so when she comes to the point of repentance, it is a glorious submission. "In this height and depth and breadth the little idea of herself which she had hitherto called *me* dropped down and vanished unfluttering, into bottomless distance, like a bird in a space without air" (*That Hideous Strength*, 394). And the angels burst into song.

All must come to Christ, but because He is at the center, it means that some come from opposite directions.

WITHER, FROST, AND STUDDOCK

The central point of *Abolition* had to do with the demolition job that a certain pernicious form of education accomplishes when consistently applied. When this form of education is set loose among the children of men, the end result is the *eradication* of men. Lewis is pointing to the difference between being educated and being erased. Nothing is more obvious at the end of the process and so hard to see at the beginning of it.

One section of *Abolition* is entitled "Men Without Chests." Man has an animal body, of course, and man also has reason. But, as Lewis points out, he also has sentiments of practical reason—the heart, the chest, the trunk. And Mark is an almost perfect example of the kind of end product that modern schools were turning out, the kind that Lewis was objecting to so strenuously in *Abolition*.

> It must be remembered that in Mark's mind hardly one rag of noble thought, either Christian or Pagan, had a secure lodging. His education had been neither scientific nor classical—merely "Modern." The severities both of abstraction and of high human tradition had passed him by: and he had neither peasant shrewdness nor aristocratic honor to help him. He was a man of straw, a glib examinee in subjects that require no exact knowledge . . . and the first hint of a real threat

to his bodily life knocked him sprawling. (*That Hideous Strength*, 226)

Set this description of Mark alongside that justly famous passage from *Abolition*:

> In a sort of ghastly simplicity we remove the organ and demand the function. We make men without chests and expect of them virtue and enterprise. We laugh at honour and are shocked to find traitors in our midst. We castrate and bid the geldings be fruitful. (*The Abolition of Man*, 26)

Mark Studdock was still in the process of his degradation, but Wither and Frost were both examples of men already long gone. They had already graduated into their eradication as men.

And Lewis had them well in hand, admirer of Bunyan as he was, when he gave them their names. When Wither realizes that all was lost, it was "incredible how little this knowledge moved him. It could not, because he had long ceased to believe in knowledge itself." And here, as Wither stood on the lip of "endless terror," it is striking that Lewis points back to the *curriculum* he had worked through. From Hegel to Hume to Pragmatism to Logical Positivism to ... the "complete void" (*That Hideous Strength*, 438).

Frost descended into epistemic madness by a different route, but it was not all *that* different.

> The nearest thing to a human passion which still existed in him was a sort of cold fury against all who believed in the mind . . . . He became able to know (and simultaneously refused the knowledge) that he had been wrong from the beginning, that souls and personal responsibility existed. He half saw: he wholly hated. (*That Hideous Strength*, 445)

And of course, in this book the focal point for all these machinations of the bad guys was the Head—a severed and detached head hooked up to tubes and dials, and with absolutely no chest at all.

These men are all metaphors for the intellectual disintegration of the West. They were pioneers of what Van Til called "integration downward into the Void."

The world has gone crazy, but there is a method in the madness. We in the West—and if you think a phrase like *the West* is a racist dog whistle, then *you* are the problem—find ourselves, as a result of our own follies and stupid choices, locked up in the Objective Room. This is the room where Mark was being trained to suppress the normal, and embrace the ultimate Dadaism of all things. He was being catechized in ultimate relativism. He was made to do things that made no sense *because* they made no sense.

Hard line conservatives see the problem more clearly than most evangelicals do, and this is even the case with members of the alt-right. But they have no plan—unless you want to call it a plan if people run around in Belbury punching people randomly. Seeing the problem is not the same thing as having a solution or cure. At the same time, the Christian church, which *has* the cure, cannot be prevailed upon to see the problem.

When we look at the contradictory things that are thrown at our heads every day, we think that they are the silly ones. Why would they say that? *That's* a contradiction. They demand that women be given safe spaces, and they also demand that transitioning men, pre-surgery, have full access to the women's showers. They demand that we agree that homosexuals are "born this way," and they also demand that we acknowledge that "gender is ultimately fluid." They insist on women's rights, while also insisting that there is no such thing as a woman.

But *they* are not the ones being tested. When Frost is having Mark do all kinds of absurd things in the Objective Room, we are not being given to understand that Frost is being tested, or that *Frost* is being evaluated. No, he is already among the damned. Mark is the one being tested, and he does not pass the test until he repents and says, "It's all bloody nonsense, and I'm damned if I do any such thing."

And we will not be saved unless and until we come to the same point, and say the same thing. The evangelical church is crammed full of men without chests, who must absolutely learn that they must come to the point of rebellion. And the evangelical church is *also* crammed with unsubmissive women, who must repent of that, seeking to learn what it is to glory in womanhood. Men can't make women submissive, and shouldn't try. But this reality doesn't make submission somehow optional. There is nothing optional about it—and it is no trifle.

Every Christian couple should resolve to follow the pattern that the Bible calls normal. Husbands should imitate Christ, in seeking to live as a sacrificial head. And women should imitate the Christ, seeking to obey their husbands in everything. What are we seeking to accomplish by this? We are trying to head off the banquet scene at Belbury.

THE CENTRALITY OF CHRIST

The point of Mark's rebellion came with the demand that he trample on a crucifix. What are you going to do with *Jesus*? When Mark rebels, he does it by identifying with Jesus as representing the side of *normal*. At this point, he had no confidence that Jesus was God—but he knew the world around him was bent, twisted, and demented, and that Jesus was a straight line in a crooked world.

Normal. What a revolutionary word. That is an incendiary word to set the world on fire. Given the state of the world today, it is going to be a pretty big grease fire, but here we are. This is what God has given us, so grease fire it is.

But you can't have normal without Jesus. And furthermore, *if* you have Jesus, that will bring you straight back to normal. Jesus and metrosexual do not go together. Jesus and artificial wombs do not go together. Jesus and VR sex do not go together. Jesus and prancing men in the offertory do not go together. Jesus and 57 genders do not go together. Virtually every outrageous thing we read about today is being served up to us from the macrobes. But we are Christians. We are to follow Jesus. We are to line up behind the Lord Jesus Christ.

If you read *Abolition of Man*, you will see Lewis's culminating point is that man's supposed "conquest" of nature is actually a radical expansion of what parts of nature are appropriate to tinker with, and when we have made mankind itself the passive subject of these perverse ministrations, we will then find out two things. The first is that man's conquest of nature actually means some men's conquest of other men, with nature as the instrument, and secondly, it means *nature's* conquest of that handful of men who thought they were now running the show. The abolition of man refers to a commitment to the ultimate plasticity of all things, such that anything can be shaped and molded according to our whims. And then it turns out that our whims are being molded and shaped from elsewhere.

This abolition of man comes through the abolition of woman, which Lewis also foretold. And he saw it all. The progressive agenda is nothing but a wrecking crew of gracious femininity—bloody wombs, barrenness as glory, perverse arts, grotesque lesbianism, and all the rest of it. *Nothing* that is tumbling down around our heads right now would be a surprise to Lewis.

We are all in this Objective Room, and some well-respected among us have decided to trample on the crucifix. Others haven't done it yet, but they are still friends with the cool kids who have "evolved" in their thinking.

But we proclaim Jesus. Not the Jesus who plays in ten thousand places, but the Jesus being preached by a hard fundamentalist prophet in a Flannery story. We preach the Jesus who turned Mark Studdock around. And we must preach Him because He is the only one who can give a man his chest back—and we have hundreds of thousands of men in dire need of one.

THE COMPANY AT ST. ANNE'S

One last point: One of the great takeaway lessons of this book, for me at any rate, and related to all the foregoing, is the greatness of insignificant service.

When Fairy Hardcastle faces the problem of finding out who Mark Studdock may have seen in his unauthorized visit to town, she has three men she needed to tail and only two men that she could assign to do the job. Those three men are Lancaster, Lyly, and Dimble, and she decided to go after the first two.

> "Both these are dangerous men. They are the sort of people who get things done—natural leaders of the other party. Dimble is quite a different type. Except that he's a Christian, there isn't really much against him."
>
> "The others know a thing or two, Lancaster particularly. In fact, he's a man we could find room for on our own side if he held the right views." (*That Hideous Strength*, 291)

Jumping to the great book by Lewis's friend Tolkien, we can see the same principle at work. In *The Two Towers*, Gandalf explains the great blind spot that was eventually the undoing of Sauron. "That we should wish to cast him down and have no one in his place is not a thought that occurs to his mind."[3] Not only so, but that hazardous mission was undertaken by two insignificant hobbits, and not by men mighty and bold.

These are good things for us to be reminded of, when we can see that the shadow from Babel's tower is as long as it ever was. In order to be

---

3. *The Two Towers* (1954; Houghton Mifflin, 2020), 485-486.

formidable adversaries to the darkness confronting us, we have to understand that we will never look formidable to *them*.

CHAPTER 10
HELL AND DAMNATION

Because the question of Hell and damnation can only be answered ultimately in the afterlife, we don't know very much about it now. And what we do know is necessarily *revealed* to us, and yet, even here it is revealed to us under various metaphors and images.

It should then be clear to us that we should be very wary about accusing people of heresy over *details* of the afterlife. For the saved it is said that it does not yet appear what we shall be like (1 John 3:2), and it seems that the same thing should go double for our understanding of the damned.

Lewis makes a careful distinction between the doctrine and the imagery that conveys the doctrine.

> A third objection turns on the frightful intensity of the pains of Hell as suggested by medieval

art and, indeed, by certain passages in Scripture. Von Hügel here warns us not to confuse the doctrine itself with the *imagery* by which it may be conveyed. (*The Problem of Pain*, 126-27)

So an image is not the same thing as the reality, but the images of Scripture are meant to convey something *about* the reality. But whenever we are dealing with symbolic language, we must remember that the symbol is always *less* than the reality. The wedding ring is less than the marriage. The flag is less than the country it represents. This means that if the lake of fire is a literal lake of fire, then it must be really bad. But if the lake of fire is merely symbolic, then that means that the reality it represents is *far worse*.

So we cannot honestly use "symbolism" to help ameliorate our existential dread of what might happen after we die. Saying that hellfire is symbolic does not make it stage fire. Saying that the fire and brimstone are symbolic does not fix our dilemma. Symbolic of *what*?

At the same time, if God wanted us to come at this subject through His inspired imagery. we must understand the images *as* images. We are therefore heretical if we deny the *fact* of damnation, but there is a good deal of room for theological work to be done on the *nature* of damnation. My discussion here assumes that universalism is out, as well as strict annihilationism. This means that damnation is a tragic reality for some, but are we talking about the damnation of human persons or *former* human persons? In short, do the inhabitants of Hell (called *helwaru* by the Anglo Saxons) still bear the image of God?

PINNING LEWIS DOWN

One of my purposes here is to show that the common idea that C.S. Lewis was a universalist is false. Now universalism is the view that everyone is eventually saved. It is also false to argue that Lewis was an annihilationist. This is the idea that the saved are saved, and that the lost at some point go completely out of existence. Damnation is temporary.

Now I believe that it can be shown that Lewis was orthodox in that he believed in the reality of an everlasting Hell, the reality of an eternal conscious torment for the damned. At the same time, I believe that he was an annihilationist *after a fashion*. I believe I can show that Lewis believed that there is eternal conscious torment for the lost soul, but that at the point of damnation the lost soul ceases to bear the image of God. Lewis believes, in short, in the eternal damnation of *former* humans, ex-people. Think of it as the ultimate and final gollumization of an individual. At some point in the process downward, Ginger ceases to be a Talking Beast.

If you bring it down the brass tacks, Lewis affirms the awful reality of Hell.

> Some will not be redeemed. There is no doctrine which I would more willingly remove from Christianity than this, if it lay in my power. But it has the full support of Scripture and, specially, of Our Lord's own words; it has always been held by Christendom; and it has the support of reason. If a game is played, it must be possible to lose it. If the happiness of a creature lies in self-surrender, no one can make that surrender but himself (though many can help him to make it) and he may refuse. (*The Problem of Pain*, 119-120)

FIRST, SOME HARD REALITIES

C.S. Lewis was not someone to trifle with the text of Scripture, or with the long history of Christian teaching on this subject. If the Lord taught something plainly, Lewis was prepared to acknowledge that fact: "But to a Christian the true tragedy of Nero must be not that he fiddled while the city was on fire but that he fiddled on the brink of hell. You must forgive me for the crude monosyllable."[1]

He goes on:

> I know that many wiser and better Christians than I in these days do not like to mention Heaven and hell even in a pulpit. I know, too, that nearly all the references to this subject in the

---

1. "Learning in Wartime," in *The Weight of Glory*, 48.

New Testament come from a single source. But then that source is Our Lord Himself. People will tell you it is St. Paul, but that is untrue. These overwhelming doctrines are dominical.[2]

This should be a self-evident observation, but somehow it is still possible to miss it. The hellfire preacher of the New Testament is Jesus, not His apostles. Not Paul. In fact Paul never mentions Hell by name once in all of his writings. He refers (from time to time) to the wrath and judgment of God, but the one who goes into the details ("send someone with a drop of water for my tongue") is Jesus. When it comes to lurid descriptions of the damned, no one in the New Testament rivals an eloquent Dublin Jesuit from 1878, but there are moments when Jesus comes close. And only Jesus.

It is quite striking that Lewis is supposed by some to be a universalist, and yet so many of his books deal with this subject. *The Great Divorce* is all about ghostly spirits teetering on the brink of a ghastly and everlasting night. *The Screwtape Letters* is a set of letters from a senior devil to a junior tempter, passing on the tricks of the trade, such that he might be able to drag his "clients" down to their "Father below."

It even comes up in his children's literature.

---

2. "Learning in Wartime," in *The Weight of Glory*, 48.

> The creatures came rushing on, their eyes brighter and brighter as they drew nearer and nearer to the standing Stars. But as they came right up to Aslan one or other of two things happened to each of them. They all looked straight in his face, I don't think they had any choice about that. And when some looked, the expression of their faces changed terribly—it was fear and hatred: except that, on the faces of Talking Beasts, the fear and hatred lasted only for a fraction of a second. You could see that they suddenly ceased to be Talking Beasts. They were just ordinary animals. And all the creatures who looked at Aslan in that way swerved to their right, his left, and disappeared into his huge black shadow, which (as you have heard) streamed away to the left of the doorway. The children never saw them again. I don't know what became of them. (*The Last Battle*, 175)

TAKING THE IMAGES SERIOUSLY

Assuming that biblical descriptions of damnation are symbolic and metaphorical, we have to do some work in harmonizing them. For example, how do we reconcile the image of an outer darkness with a lake of fire?

> Our Lord speaks of Hell under three symbols: first, that of punishment ("everlasting punishment," Matthew 25:46); second, that of destruc-

tion ("fear Him who is able to destroy both body and soul in Hell," Matthew 10:28); and thirdly, that of privation, exclusion, or banishment into "the darkness outside," as in the parables of the man without a wedding garment or of the wise and foolish virgins. The prevalent image of fire is significant because it combines the ideas of torment and destruction. Now it is quite certain that all these expressions are intended to suggest something unspeakably horrible, and any interpretation which does not face that fact is, I am afraid, out of court from the beginning. (*The Problem of Pain*, 126-27)

Lewis here sees that the point of this language is to make us recoil from the prospect of being damned. But if absolute annihilation lies in the future for some, then this means that Christian damnation is equivalent to Buddhist salvation. But that is not "unspeakably horrible."

The three characteristics of damnation that Lewis points out are punishment, destruction, and exclusion or exile. Because we are talking about the final or ultimate things, this would mean ultimate punishment, ultimate destruction, and ultimate exclusion. But how can these three things exist together without one of them swallowing up the other two? And how could any of them be applied to a finite human being without it swallowing him up?

To make this point clear, everlasting torment in fire is not something that a human being could endure without going totally and completely mad. But perhaps that final insanity *is* the damnation.

> Burn a log, and you have gases, heat and ash. To *have been* a log means now being those three things. If souls can be destroyed, must there not be a state of *having been* a human soul? And is not that, perhaps, the state which is equally well described as torment, destruction, and privation? You will remember that in the parable, the saved go to a place prepared for *them*, while the damned go to a place never made for men at all. To enter heaven is to become more human than you ever succeeded in being on earth; to enter hell, is to be banished from humanity. What is cast (or casts itself) into hell is not a man: it is "remains." To be a complete man means to have the passions obedient to the will and the will offered to God: to *have been* a man—to be an ex-man or "damned ghost"—would presumably mean to consist of a will utterly centred in its self and passions utterly uncontrolled by the will. It is, of course, impossible to imagine what the consciousness of such a creature—already a loose congeries of mutually antagonistic sins rather than a sinner—would be like. (*The Problem of Pain*, 127-28)

In *The Great Divorce*, Lewis has the fictional version of his mentor, George MacDonald, point at this from another direction.

> The question is whether she is a grumbler, or only a grumble. If there is a real woman—even the least trace of one—still there inside the grumbling, it can be brought to life again. If there's one wee spark under all those ashes, we'll blow it till the whole pile is red and clear. But if there's nothing but ashes we'll not go on blowing them in our own eyes forever. They must be swept up.[3]

A QUESTION OF SIZE

George MacDonald was in many ways a mentor to Lewis. It was a book by MacDonald that first baptized Lewis's imagination, and he thought so much of his wisdom that he collected a number of MacDonald's sayings and published them in an anthology. But MacDonald was heterodox on the subject of Hell (he was a universalist), and so in *The Great Divorce* Lewis places MacDonald as a guide to the protagonist, and one of the things he explains is the coming damnation of the lost. In short, Lewis fixes MacDonald's theology in the afterlife for him.

"'In your own books, Sir,' said I, 'you were a Universalist. You talked as if all men would be saved. And St. Paul too.'"

---

3. *The Great Divorce* (1945; New York: Collier Books, 2018), 77.

But then Lewis punts. "All answers deceive" (*The Great Divorce,* 140). He doesn't *quite* fix everything.

However, notice something else he does. MacDonald points out that a tiny crack in the ground, or one very much like it, is where all of Hell is located.

> "All Hell is smaller than one pebble of your earthly world: but it is smaller than one atom of *this* world, the Real World. Look at yon butterfly. If it swallowed all Hell, Hell would not be big enough to do it any harm or to have any taste."
>
> "It seems big enough when you're in it, Sir."
>
> "And yet all loneliness, angers, hatreds, envies and itchings that it contains, if rolled into one single experience and put into the scale against the least moment of the joy that is felt by the least in Heaven, would have no weight that could be registered at all." (*The Great Divorce,* 138)

So Lewis doesn't believe in "no Hell." He believes that from the perspective of Heaven, there is *almost* no Hell. And from the perspective of Hell, there is nothing *but* Hell: "For a damned soul is nearly nothing: it is shrunk, shut up in itself" (*The Great Divorce,* 139).

A RETROACTIVE ESCHATON

So from the heavenly aspect, Hell shrinks. But it grows for those who are trapped in and by it. Not only does Hell grow in their (shrunk) experience, it also grows backwards through time: "But ye can get some likeness of it if ye say that both good and evil, when they are full grown, become retrospective" (*The Great Divorce*, 69).

Lewis argues that, for the damned, there is nothing left that could be a consolation—not even memories. Say that a lost soul had a very comfortable life. In his torment, he would not be able to look back on that with any kind of fondness. The experience of damnation works backward through time, corrupting everything. For the lost, there is nothing left that is good.

The same thing is true for the redeemed. The experience of Heaven works backward, cleansing everything. Every tear will be wiped away—including the tears we shed *here*.

THE MIND OF HELL

The late journalist and author Ralph de Toledano once had a back and forth with the editor of one of his books. He had capitalized Hell in the book, and when the proofs came back, the *H*'s for Heaven and Hell had all been put in the lower case. De Toledano restored them all and then sent the manuscript back again. "Why did you capitalize Hell?" his editor wanted to know. "Because," de Toledano said, "they're *places*. You know, like Scarsdale."

So everyone who believes in the teaching of Scripture knows that Heaven and Hell are actual *places*, and people are actually consigned there. By the judgment of God they are consigned there. But we make a serious mistake when we think that the location is what makes the Hell. The damned could be sent anywhere and they would bring the Hell with them. Hell is the kind of place that wraps around the hellish thought.

And so what kind of people are these?

> "There are only two kinds of people in the end: those who say to God, 'Thy will be done,' and those to whom God says, in the end, 'Thy will be done.' All that are in Hell, choose it." (*The Great Divorce*, 75)

> I willingly believe that the damned are, in one sense, successful, rebels to the end; that the doors of hell are locked on the *inside*. (*The Problem of Pain*, 130)

For these lost souls, Heaven would be a greater torment for them than Hell is. The essence of their rebellion is that they do not want to be with God. Heaven is suffused with that glorious presence, and they would want nothing but *out*.

Allow an absurd thought experiment for a moment. Suppose that 10,000 years into their damnation, one of the *helwaru* genuinely repented. We know that this will not happen because the judgment is to eternal fire. But why it is an eternal fire? *Why* is the damnation eternal? The damnation is eternal because the sinning is eternal. Damnation is eternal because—despite the agony—the lack of repentance is robust and ongoing. Because repentance is a gift of God, this means that if someone in Hell were to repent, Hell *could* not contain them.

Hell is not the result of God losing all sense of proportion, condemning someone to eternal flames because they used to cheat at pinochle. Rather, the judgment of God falls on someone because of *their* complete loss of all sense of proportion. The damnation is eternal because the lack of repentance is eternal.

While I don't support this variant reading in the gospel of Mark, it nevertheless sums up the situation nicely. Eternal judgment maps onto eternal sin. But "whoever blasphemes against the Holy Spirit never has forgiveness, but is guilty of an eternal sin" (Mark 3:29, ESV).

And we should not accept the charge that this makes all the inhabitants of Heaven heartless and cruel. They know that the judge of the whole earth has done right, as Abraham knew, and they can rest in the fact that there is no injustice in the sentences that have been passed. Indeed, the sentences are nothing *but* justice.

> The demand of the loveless and the self-imprisoned that they should be allowed to blackmail the

universe: that till they consent to be happy (on their own terms) no one else shall taste joy: that theirs should be the final power; that Hell should be able to *veto* Heaven. (*The Great Divorce*, 135)

Nevertheless, as Lewis expressed it in one of his poems, however infinite the judgment might feel to those experiencing it, God has placed fixed boundaries to the suffering.

> God in His mercy made
> The fixed pains of Hell.
> That misery might be stayed,
> God in His mercy made
> Eternal bounds and bade
> Its waves no further swell.
> God in his mercy made
> The fixed pains of Hell.[4]

---

4. "Divine Justice," in *Poems* (1964; New York: Harper Collins, 2017), 152

CHAPTER 11
TONGUES OF ANGELS

In his essay "Transposition," C.S. Lewis begins by seeking to treat the subject of *glossolalia*, or speaking in tongues, and he does this by discussing a much larger subject—how the reduction valve has to work when a more complex system of thought is translated into a simpler system.

He does an astonishing job of explaining how higher levels of thought cannot be translated into a lower without one or more elements of the lower being pressed into some form of double duty. The insight is an essential one, in my view, for understanding what it means to be human—but it is unfortunately marred with what I see as an unfortunate inconsistency in the argument.

Transposition is what *has* to happen when a more complex reality has to be translated into a lesser. For example, the three-dimensional world around us can be reproduced by a pencil on white paper, but when this is done, some of the lines will have to do more than one thing. An acute angle has to be used to represent both a triangle in the real world, as well as parallel lines meeting in the distance. And if a language with fifteen distinct vowel sounds is to be translated into a language that has only five distinct symbols for vowel sounds, this means that some of the symbols in the receiving language will have to do more than one thing. Lewis uses illustrations like this to explain how a higher spiritual reality will have to use certain physiological reactions in us in such a way as that *they* mean more than just one thing. Lewis explains how his physiological reaction to bad news is identical to his reaction of aesthetic delight—a fluttering in the diaphragm.

His starting point for his discussion is the gift of tongues bestowed at the first Christian Pentecost, and this is what sets up the problem for him. The inconsistency that I would want to identify has to do with what category Lewis places *glossolalia* in. What does he believe *actually* happened on the first Pentecost? I raise the question because he appears to place the phenomenon into two completely different categories.

In the first instance, he grants the miraculous nature of the gift of tongues in Acts 2, noting accurately that the languages spoken were known and understood by others present. The miracle consisted, not in the nature of the language spoken, but rather in the fact that acquisition of the language was an instantaneous gift. For example, Parthians heard the praises of God being declared in their native language by someone who had never studied or learned their native language (Acts 2:9). Thus far my understanding lines up with what Lewis believes.

> On the other hand, we cannot as Christians shelve the story of Pentecost or deny that there, at any rate, the speaking with tongues was miraculous. For the men spoke not gibberish but languages unknown to them, though known to other people present.[1]

With this understanding, there is no need for transposition whatever.

But the odd thing, however, is that Lewis then goes on to identify this gift of tongues at Pentecost with a very common recurring religious phenomenon, one which *would* require transposition to keep it from being more than just a kind of jabbering in the grip of a religious hysteria.

So the first explanation is that God gave the unstudied gift of grammar, syntax and vocabulary to recipients who then spoke in a new language that they had not known when they had first awakened

---

1. "Transposition," in *The Weight of Glory*, 92–93.

that morning. So this explanation is that the divine gift of tongues was the gift of an unstudied language, while the oddments of religious experience that many of us have witnessed are something else entirely. I do not see how there is any pressing need to identify the two phenomena. They appear to me to be completely different. But then Lewis appears to blend them together.

> On the one hand, *glossolalia* has remained an intermittent "variety of religious experience" down to the present day. Every now and then we hear that in some revivalist meeting one or more of those present has burst into a torrent of what appears to be gibberish.[2]

This inconsistency is really an odd one. Lewis in one place says that the gift was the gift of an actual language, and yet he also seems to say that what the disciples did on that first Pentecost was the same kind of thing that happens when someone in the modern world has a case of religious hysterics. If that latter instance were the case, then something like transposition would be necessary in order to salvage it. Lewis acknowledged earlier that this was not what happened, but later on he appears to change course.

---

2. "Transposition," in *The Weight of Glory*, 92.

> Those who spoke with tongues, as St. Paul did, can well understand how that holy phenomenon differed from the hysterical phenomenon—although be it remembered, they were in a sense exactly the same phenomenon.[3]

Exactly the same phenomenon? In other words, Lewis is saying that examined from the outside, the early Christians were speaking gibberish in just the same way that some mystic at a revival meeting starts combining syllables randomly. An outside observer would not be able to tell the difference between jumbled syllables and articulate expression.

But a visiting Egyptian to Jerusalem on Pentecost *could* tell the difference. He could understand what the disciple speaking his language was saying, even if the man speaking it could not have done anything comparable to this the day before. If it was just hysterics, then how could the Egyptian understand it? If it were *not* hysterics, but was saved from that fate by transposition (which happened *inside* the mind of the person with the gift of tongues), the question still remains. How could the Egyptian understand it if externally it was gibberish?

So Lewis appears to be saying that God gave gibberish, as far as the appearances went, but internally the recipient knew that he was not speaking

---

3. "Transposition," in *The Weight of Glory*, 105.

gibberish *really*. On the inside, he was speaking Egyptian. But the problem is that the text says that he was speaking Egyptian on the outside also, in a way that the Egyptians could understand.

Suppose we were to say something in English like "in the beginning God created heaven and earth." In Latin, this would be *in principio Deus creavit caelum et terram*. Now suppose that someone else in a frenzy says something like "bah bah bah shambalah na na." There is basically only one vowel sound in all of that, and they are all stirred up together like they were vegetables in a sizzling wok, separated from one another by only three consonants. This is not a language at all, and hence there is no need to call on Lewis's ingenious proposal of transposition to explain anything.

In short, I believe that Lewis is exactly right about how transposition occurs whenever a higher form of thought is translated into a lower, but transposition doesn't work at all when a higher form of thought is translated into gibberish. In other words, once any kind of thought is "translated" into gibberish, it isn't a higher form of thought any more because it isn't thought at all. And hence it isn't translation at all.

If the archangel Michael were to translate a poem he wrote about the heavenly glories that he knew about into pidgin English, then the doctrine of transposition *would* be necessary to describe what was going on. But if the whole poem were to be dumped into a big box of Scrabble pieces, randomly thrown together, there wouldn't be transposition at all. This is because there wouldn't be translation at all. We have annihilated the angelic poem; we have not rendered it into a more limited and lower register.

Now at Pentecost it is likely that transposition as Lewis describes it *was* in fact occurring because God was inspiring the early disciples to speak in accordance with what the Holy Spirit was moving them to say. What the Spirit was thinking, and what the languages they were speaking in were capable of rendering, were of necessity operating on two different levels. But that lower level was still made up of languages—each with grammar, syntax, vocabulary, etc.

"And they were all filled with the Holy Ghost, and began to speak with other tongues, as the Spirit gave them utterance" (Acts 2:4).

The word for tongues here is *glossais*. This word is being used interchangeably with *dialekto*, the word in the following verses from which we get our word *dialect*.

"Now when this was noised abroad, the multitude came together, and were confounded, because that every man heard them speak in his own language" (Acts 2:6).

"And how hear we every man in our own tongue, wherein we were born?" (Acts 2:8).

Often what appears to be gibberish in the modern era has this appearance because it *is* in fact gibberish. As mentioned above, a language has grammar, vocabulary, syntax. If someone says *shambalala* a number of times, this does not appear to have any syntax at all—and thus it has no need of Lewis's wonderful insight about transposition.

C.S. Lewis is mistaken here, as I have argued, but I believe the mistake is borne of two characteristic Lewisian virtues, both of them having to do with his humility. The first is to discount the value of his own preferences if he suspects that he is in any way embarrassed by something he should not be embarrassed by. In this case, he represents himself as a stodgy Anglican who doesn't quite know what to do with the kind of religious excitement that is capable of bursting out in tongues. And on the other side, he is consistently eager to believe the best about the religious experiences of others, and so he used his unique gifts to provide a modern tongues-speaker with a glorious argument that he didn't really need.

But we needed the argument, and are happy to profit from it.

CHAPTER 12
CHILDREN WITHOUT CHESTS

If adults are wandering around, not knowing who they are, or what they are supposed to be doing, the chances are excellent that as children they were not taught who they were, or what they were supposed to be doing. As one observer has noted, education is about formation, not just information.

Lewis recognizes the importance of this, and begins his wonderful little book *The Abolition of Man* with a statement about the foundational importance of objective truth in education. He begins with these words: "I doubt whether we are sufficiently attentive to the importance of elementary text-books" (*The Abolition of Man*, 1).

What drew his attention was a passing comment in a children's textbook that said that when we say something is "sublime" we are not really saying anything that is objectively true about realities external to ourselves. Lewis saw the coming storm of subjectivism when it was a mere cloud the size of a man's fist. We are in the middle of a subjective hurricane, and we still want to identify it as a sunny day. "The authors themselves, I suspect, hardly know what they are doing to the boy, and he cannot know what is being done to him" (*The Abolition of Man*, 5).

Because they were instilling subjective relativism in a world that was largely still held together by the previous Christian consensus, the authors of this textbook could assume that there was no way the world would fall apart because of what they were teaching. The force of that Christian consensus could be assumed as being simply the way "the world is," and the subjectivism they were promoting would then be at liberty to run around the edges of an inherently stable world. The world was to remain stable all by itself somehow.

But the poison they were administered was more hazardous than that.

> That is their day's lesson in English, though of English they have learned nothing. Another little portion of the human heritage has been quietly taken from them before they were old enough to understand. (*The Abolition of Man*, 11)

But what are the young students getting *instead* of an education in English? They are getting indoctrinated in the assumptions of relativism, they were being schooled in the default assumptions of subjectivism. And it was an education that collapsed as soon as any weight was put on it.

It is an "education" in the *feels*, and where Lewis saw the ramifications of that little cloud the size of a man's fist, and could see it clearly, we are living in the middle of the typhoon, and cannot see a blessed thing.

And this brings us to the quote that must be remembered, the quote that makes *Abolition* a book worth reading.

> And all the time—such is the tragi-comedy of our situation—we continue to clamour for those very qualities we are rendering impossible. You can hardly open a periodical without coming across the statement that what our civilization needs is more "drive," or dynamism, or self-sacrifice, or "creativity." In a sort of ghastly simplicity we remove the organ and demand the function. We make men without chests and expect of them virtue and enterprise. We laugh at honour and are shocked to find traitors in our midst. We castrate and bid the geldings be fruitful. (*The Abolition of Man*, 27)

The Abolition of Man and *That Hideous Strength* were composed right around the same time, and both of them were aimed at the same target. "This is a 'tall story' about devilry, though it has behind it a serious 'point' which I have tried to make in my *Abolition of Man*" (*That Hideous Strength*, 7).

Lewis is arguing (in both books) that men can be described as having three important component parts. There is the head, which would be reason. There is the stomach and sex organs, which would be the animal appetites. Some assume that this is it, and whichever one wins that particular wrestling match determines what kind of person the person will be.

But Lewis identifies a third part, one which he calls the chest. This is where a person's *sentiments* are. This is the home of his foundational *loyalties*. And it is absolutely essential that the process of education inculcate sentiments in the chest that are just, noble, right, proper, and good. If the "chest" is allowed to atrophy, the result is that the appetites will win over reason every time. Reason will simply become a tool that the appetites will seize as a means of rationalizing their way to whatever it is they want.

Now Mark Studdock is an alum of the kind of educational system that Lewis is objecting to so violently. Studdock is the product of this way of teaching. And this is why he still needs to become a person—something his education did not help him with.

> From now onwards till the moment of final decision should meet him, the different men in him appeared with startling rapidity and each seemed very complete while it lasted. Thus, skidding violently from one side to the other, his youth approached the moment at which he would begin to be a person. (*That Hideous Strength*, 266)

This is result of being taught by instructors who occupy the seat of scoffers. When a student like Mark is being taught by instructors who have taken in the demeanor of debunking, the problem is not that they debunk *this* hero, or puncture the glory of *that* particular myth. The problem with the scoffer is that his attitude is a universal corrosive, and eats out every container you might try to keep it in.

And debunkers often have the good sense to start with heroes who really *did* have feet of clay, and so half the work of debunking is already done for them. But more is being torn down than just this statue of Thomas Jefferson, or that mural of Christopher Columbus. They are the immediate target, but the ultimate target is the permanent things.

So if we are seeking to advance the Lewis project, as we should be seeking to do, the charge should be to invest, wherever you can, in the permanent things. And the permanent things include more than Platonic geometry. They also include the tenets of practical reason—ethics, in other words.

> From the Stoic and Confucian, "do not do to others what you would not like them to do to you"; to the Christian, "Do as you would be done by" is a real advance. The morality of Nietzsche is a mere innovation. The first is an advance because no one who did not admit the validity of the old maxim could see reason for accepting the new one, and anyone who accepted the old would at once recognize the new as an extension of the same principle . . . . But the Nietzschean ethic can be accepted only if we are ready to scrap traditional morals as a mere error and then to put ourselves in a position where we can find no ground for any value judgments at all. It is the difference between a man who says to us: "You like your vegetables moderately fresh; why not grow your own and have them perfectly fresh?" and a man who say, "Throw away that loaf and try eating bricks and centipedes instead."[1]

And for those who believe that this will result in a culture that is necessarily stagnant, we may answer the jibe with an appeal to actual geometry.

> Space does not stink because it has preserved its three dimensions from the beginning. The square on the hypotenuse has not gone mouldy

---

1. "The Poison of Subjectivism," in *Christian Reflection*, 76-77.

by continuing to equal the sum of the squares of the other two sides.[2]

C.S. Lewis was not just a winsome and engaging writer, a popularizer of theological topics. He was also a prophetic writer who saw and understood the foundational issues that continue to roil us in our culture wars over half a century later.

For a striking example, in *That Hideous Strength*, Ransom says this about the inhabitants of Sulva, our moon.

> "On this side, the womb is barren and the marriages are cold. There dwell an accursed people, full of pride and lust. There when a young man takes a maiden in marriage, they do not lie together, but each lies with a cunningly fashioned image of the other, made to move and to be warm by devilish arts, for real flesh will not please them, they are so dainty (*delicati*) in their dreams of lust. Their real children they fabricate by vile arts in a secret place." (*That Hideous Strength*, 337)

The contrast with the biblical approach is stark.

"Finally, brethren, whatsoever things are true, whatsoever things are honest, whatsoever things are just, whatsoever things are pure, whatsoever things

---

2. "The Poison of Subjectivism," in *Christian Reflection*, 76.

are lovely, whatsoever things are of good report; if there be any virtue, and if there be any praise, think on these things" (Phil. 4:8).

Accept this principle, and do as you please. But we must not accept this principle woodenly, or with eyes tight shut, which leads to the next point. Following Augustine, our affections must be *ordered* affections. We cannot simply line things up in a row, and number off the good ones, and pay attention to those. The world is more complicated than that.

Let us take the old order of liberal arts, mechanical arts, and the fine arts. Our problem is that we have removed theology as the queen of the sciences in the liberal arts, and then we separated the mechanical arts and the fine arts from their decapitated mother. The mechanical arts enable STEM graduates to head out into the world in order to build another bridge. The fine arts enable graduates to head off to Manhattan in order to cop a pose at wine and cheese soirees at museum showings. Mechanical arts (e.g. engineering) and the fine arts (e.g. painting) both must be oriented to something greater than themselves, and the liberal arts, the compass by which they are to be oriented, must itself have a needle in it.

Lewis hated the rot that subjectivism brought with it, and brought with it necessarily. But in order to avoid that rot, there must be something fixed, something permanent, something transcendent. Consider what Lewis says about the function of literature.

> Literature exists to teach what is useful, to honour what deserves honour, to appreciate what is delightful. The useful, honourable, and delightful things are superior to it: it exists for their sake; its own use, honour, or delightfulness is derivative from theirs. (*The Discarded Image*, 214)

Now words like useful, honorable, and delightful are words that ultimately have to point to the heavens. Unless they can point to the heavens, they have no weight within themselves. They have no self-generating authority.

Now when the anchor of the permanent things is removed, what happens? The mechanical arts veer into devilish engineering—the severed Head from *That Hideous Strength* hooked up to tubes and dials. And when the fine arts are detached from the permanent things, they deteriorate into the grotesque or the absurd. The become the kind of cartoonish Clevers that Lewis lampooned so effectively in *The Pilgrim's Regress*.

The ancients thought that each man was the cosmos in microcosm, and whether that is the case or not, it will serve for the concluding illustration. In *Abolition of Man*, Lewis argues that "the chest" is the place where the sentiments or the affections lie, and he says that it is here that we need to find our protection from the rot of relativism. The whole man must serve God, from the head to the loins, and the chest in between. But it is useless, he showed, to try to do this without the chest.

I would urge us all to consider that our entire culture is "without a chest." That missing chest is the liberal arts, with theology in her rightful place. And I would suggest further that it was Lewis's understanding of this that has made him such a potent cultural apologist. He is the apologist for our time.

CHAPTER 13

LEWIS AND THE ECCENTRIC CREATIONIST

One of the things that is distressing to conservative Christians who appreciate the weight of Lewis's apologetic contributions to a robust defense of the Christian faith is the fact that Lewis was apparently at peace with theistic evolution. Given how far down *that* road we now are, this appears to many to be a fatal deficiency in Lewis. I want to acknowledge that there were some significant problems in this area, but that some additional factors have to be taken into consideration. When all of these factors are considered, that word *fatal* will have to be removed from the phrase "fatal deficiency."

THREE OPTIONS

Given the statements in some of his books, there are three basic views concerning Lewis and his relationship to Darwin's theory of evolution. The first is that he was simply a theistic evolutionist, and we need to deal with it. Michael Peterson represents this view well. "Lewis himself embraced a more standard form of theistic evolution, or we might say, Christian theistic evolution."[1]

The second view is that he rejected theistic evolution for most of his life, but that he was willing to say that theistic evolution was not *necessarily* inconsistent with the Christian faith. His seeming accommodations with the theory were, *arguendo*, simply provisional, for the sake of argument. In other words, Lewis did not want to get distracted from what he believed to be the main issue, and *his* central task, a defense of the basic truths of orthodox Christianity. This second view is the perspective taken by Jerry Bergman.[2]

The third view is that he was a heretical or renegade theistic evolutionist after his conversion to Christianity, and that later in his life, and especially during the 1950s, he became increasingly skeptical about the central Darwinian claims. This is the view I am taking here.

---

1. Michael Peterson, *C.S. Lewis and the Christian Worldview* (Oxford; OUP, 2020), 132.
2. Jerry Bergman, *C.S. Lewis, Anti-Darwinist: A Careful Examination of the Development of His Views on Darwinism* (Eugene, OR: Wipf and Stock, 2016).

THE EARLY LEWIS

His accommodation with evolution appears particularly pronounced in early books like *The Problem of Pain*, where our hominoid and pre-Adamite ancestors appear to be simply assumed. Taken at face value, this is a significant problem, and cannot really be glossed over.

The following, taken from *The Problem of Pain*, seems to me to simply accept the Darwinian account, and not just for the sake of argument:

> For long centuries God perfected the animal form which was to become the vehicle of humanity and the image of Himself. He gave it hands whose thumb could be applied to each of the fingers, and jaws and teeth and throat capable of articulation, and a brain sufficiently complex to execute all the material motions whereby rational thought is incarnated. The creature may have existed for ages in this state before it became man: it may even have been clever enough to make things which a modern archaeologist would accept as proof of its humanity. But it was only an animal because all its physical and psychical processes were directed to purely material and natural ends. Then, in the fullness of time, God caused to descend upon this organism, both on its psychology and physiology, a new kind of consciousness which could say "I" and "me," which could look upon itself as an ob-

ject, which knew God, which could make judgements of truth, beauty, and goodness, and which was so far above time that it could perceive time flowing past. (*The Problem of Pain*, 72)

And so there you have it.

EVOLUTION FRAYED

But we need to remember that *The Problem of Pain* was published in 1940. Lewis was converted to the Christian faith just 9 years before this, in 1931. He died in 1963, many years after the publication of this work. Was there any subsequent (sorry) evolution in his thinking on this subject over the course of his Christian life? I think we have more than enough evidence to answer that question affirmatively.

The book *Christian Reflections* contains the great essay "The Funeral of a Great Myth." That essay was published in 1945, and gives us solid grounds for believing that Lewis was growing increasingly disenchanted with all things evolutionary. Speaking of evolution as a worldview, Lewis says this: "It gives us almost everything the imagination craves—irony, heroism, vastness, unity in multiplicity, and a tragic close. It appeals to every part of me except my reason."[3]

It is true that earlier in the essay, Lewis does the same kind of thing that he does elsewhere, which is

---

3. "The Funeral of a Great Myth," in *Christian Reflections*, 93.

to distinguish sharply between evolution as a theorem in biology, held by working (real) scientists, and evolution as an account of all things, which he is identifying as a myth. A great myth, but a myth nonetheless. But even here, Lewis is less than stalwart in the view he takes of that theorem in biology: "It may be shown, by later biologists, to be a less satisfactory hypothesis than was hoped fifty years ago."[4]

In other words, he held that evolution as a theory in biology should be given a place of respect, like all legitimate theories, but that it could be replaced down the road by subsequent evidence. If someone maintains, as a matter of faith, that it would not be possible for subsequent evidence to arise that would falsify evolution, then that person is speaking as a religious devotee, and not as a scientist. In sum, Lewis held that evolution as a myth was a noble but false mythic ideal, and that evolution as a biological theorem was a legitimate scientific theory, but that *it* might well be proven wrong at some point.

THE ACWORTH ERA

In addition, at some time in the 1940s, Lewis became acquainted with a somewhat eccentric and ardent creationist named Bernard Acworth. In calling him eccentric I am not impugning his intelligence, character, or integrity, and I think we may

---

4. "The Funeral of a Great Myth," in *Christian Reflections*, 83.

be assured that someone of Lewis's intellectual caliber and spiritual good sense would not have made friends with a crackpot *simpliciter*. The fact is that Lewis was not just dealing with Acworth as he might have done with a tedious correspondent. In the first of ten surviving letters to Acworth from Lewis, Lewis extends a cordial invitation to put Acworth up when he was visiting town. And according to Acworth's son, this was hospitality that Acworth accepted more than once. So Acworth and Lewis were acquaintances, and also friends.

Acworth had become an ardent creationist by the 1930s, and after he made his acquaintance with Lewis, he tried to persuade Lewis to throw in his lot with the creationists openly. On one occasion he tried (unsuccessfully) to get Lewis to write the preface to one of his books. Lewis replied to him in this way:

> No, I'm afraid. I shd. lose much and you wd. gain almost nothing by my writing you a preface. No one who is in doubt about your views on Darwin wd. be impressed by testimony from me, who am known to be no scientist. Many who have been or are being moved towards Christianity by my books would be deterred by finding that I was connected with anti-Darwinism.
>
> I hope (but who knows himself!) that I wd. not allow myself to be influenced by this consideration if it were only my personal concerns as

an author that was endangered. But the cause I stand for wd. be endangered too. When a man has become a popular Apologist he must watch his step. Everyone is on the look out for things that might discredit him. Sorry.[5]

This certainly looks like Lewis is simply being polite to someone who had made a somewhat brash request of him. Doesn't Lewis make it clear that he didn't want to be publicly associated with anti-Darwinism? And so why am I trying to associate him with it now?

But this letter was dated October 4, 1951, and it is likely that Acworth was emboldened to make this request by the response he had received from Lewis the previous month (September 13, 1951). Acworth had sent him a manuscript, likely for the book he was seeking the preface for. The manuscript was probably for Acworth's unpublished book, *The Lie of Evolution*. This was the response Lewis wrote to him, which should be read carefully.

> I have read nearly the whole of *Evolution* and am glad you sent it. I must confess it has shaken me: not in my belief in evolution, which was of the vaguest and most intermittent kind, but in my belief that the question was wholly unimportant.
> I wish I was younger. What inclines me now to

---

5. *The Collected Letters of C.S. Lewis*, Vol. 3, 140-141 [letter to Bernard Acworth, October 4, 1951].

think that you may be right in regarding it as *the* central and radical lie in the whole web of falsehood that now governs our lives is not so much your arguments against it as the fanatical and twisted attitudes of its defenders. The section on Anthropology was especially good . . . The point that the whole economy of nature demands *simultaneity* of at least a v.[ery] great many species is a v.[ery] strong one. Thanks: and blessings.[6]

Remember that Lewis thought that whether theistic evolution was true or not, it was possible to hold that position and remain an orthodox Christian. It was not an important issue. Here he confesses that Acworth has *shaken* him in that view. He also says that his commitment to evolution was only of the "vaguest and most intermittent kind." He wishes that he were younger so that he might have the time to delve into the issue seriously. And he says that at the center of evolutionary theory is a radical lie. All of this has to be taken into account when evaluating Lewis on Darwin. It is *false* to say that he was simply a "theistic evolutionist."

A couple of years later, after the purported missing link, the Piltdown Man, was discovered to have been a fraud, Lewis wrote this to Acworth about the exposed hoax.

---

6. *The Collected Letters of C.S. Lewis, Vol. 3*, 138 [letter to Bernard Ackworth, September 13, 1953].

> I can't help sharing a sort of glee with you about the explosion of poor old Piltdown: but I hope no one on the other side will rush in and try to exploit it . . . . But of course one inevitably feels what fun it would be if this were only the beginning of a landslide.[7]

Lewis, with his characteristic humility of mind, reminded Acworth that Christian history had contributed not a small number of fraudsters, and so we should be wary. But still, the exposure of the Piltdown fraud filled Lewis with "a sort of glee." This is not a man who was invested in the truth of the evolutionary account. And he goes on to say that if there were to be a landslide of similar exposures of evolutionary evidences, Lewis's response would be along the lines of "what fun."

And then in 1954, in a private letter to Dorothy Sayers,[8] Lewis wrote a delightful send-up of evolutionary pretensions.

> Lead us, Evolution, lead us
>   Up the future's endless stair,
> Chop us, change us, prod us, weed us,
>   For stagnation is despair:

---

7. Gary Ferngren and Ronald Numbers, "C. S. Lewis on Creation and Evolution: The Acworth Letters, 1944-1960," in *Perspectives on Science and the Christian Faith* (1996): 9.

8. Peterson, *C.S. Lewis and the Christian Worldview*, 134.

> Groping, guessing, yet progressing,
> Lead us nobody-knows-where.[9]

This is not the demeanor of a true believer in the true evolutionary faith. The cumulative evidence is devastating to the idea that Lewis was comfortable with theistic evolution. He simply was not, and at many key places he was openly hostile to it. This hostility clearly grew over time.

THE BAD EVOLUTIONIST

And in conclusion, I would also argue that during the earlier time Lewis spent as a (recovering?) theistic evolutionist, it is clear from his writing that he was a Darwinian heretic—saying and teaching things that simply don't fit with the fundamental compromise represented by theistic evolution. His doubts about certain key features of this system began even before his conversion, and indeed those doubts were part of his conversion. Those reasons are covered in detail in another chapter in this volume.[10]

By the end of his life, I don't believe we can call Lewis an evolutionist at all. And throughout the course of his career as an apologist, I believe we must say that he was a very bad one.

---

9. *The Collected Letters of C.S. Lewis, Vol. 3*, 435 [letter to Dorothy Sayers, April 3, 1954].

10. See Chapter 4.

www.ingramcontent.com/pod-product-compliance
Lightning Source LLC
LaVergne TN
LVHW041332080426
835512LV00006B/423